HOW TO SAY NO

ANCIENT WISDOM FOR MODERN READERS

■ ■ ■ ■ ■

HOW TO SAY NO

■ ■ ■ ■ ■ ■

An Ancient Guide to the Art of Cynicism

Diogenes and the Cynics

Selected, translated, and introduced by M. D. Usher

PRINCETON UNIVERSITY PRESS

PRINCETON AND OXFORD

Published by Princeton University Press
41 William Street, Princeton, New Jersey 08540
99 Banbury Road, Oxford OX2 6JX

press.princeton.edu

All Rights Reserved

Library of Congress Cataloging-in-Publication Data

Names: Diogenes, -approximately 323 B.C., author. | Usher, M. D. (Mark David), 1966– translator.
Title: How to say no : an ancient guide to the art of cynicism / Diogenes and the cynics ; selected, translated and introduced by M.D. Usher.
Description: Princeton : Princeton University Press, [2022] | Series: Ancient wisdom for modern readers | Includes bibliographical references.
Identifiers: LCCN 2022006920 (print) | LCCN 2022006921 (ebook) | ISBN 9780691229850 | ISBN 9780691229867 (ebook)
Subjects: LCSH: Cynics (Greek philosophy) | BISAC: PHILOSOPHY / History & Surveys / Ancient & Classical | PHILOSOPHY / Ethics & Moral Philosophy
Classification: LCC B508 .D56 2022 (print) | LCC B508 (ebook) | DDC 180—dc23/eng/20220218
LC record available at https://lccn.loc.gov/2022006920
LC ebook record available at https://lccn.loc.gov/2022006921

British Library Cataloging-in-Publication Data is available

Editorial: Rob Tempio and Chloe Coy
Production Editorial: Mark Bellis
Text Design: Pamela Schnitter
Jacket Design: Heather Hansen
Production: Erin Suydam
Publicity: Maria Whelan and Carmen Jimenez
Copyeditor: Lachlan Brooks

Jacket Credit: Philosopher Diogenes Sculpture/recebin/Shutterstock

This book has been composed in Stempel Garamond LT Std

Printed on acid-free paper. ∞

Printed in the United States of America

1 3 5 7 9 10 8 6 4 2

I like the sayers of No better than the sayers of Yes.

—Ralph Waldo Emerson, *Journals* Vol. 3, p. 122

CONTENTS

Doggerel (A Sonnet)

Life is a dog and then you die. Day in
day out of bed you're rung, bite back a yawn,
or nip a tick or two of sleep ere when
you shake and roll awake your groggy brawn;
you at the mirror paw: two sunken jowls,
one wispy, tonsured head, soon brushed away.
You speak!—in rueful, apathetic howls,
forever hunched at desk to sit and stay.
You play as dead and fawn like pup supine,
unbarked; you beg then defecate the dollar,
then, weary, wag your head, for more to pine.
Clad in dogtooth, choked with Oxford collar—
  like Hades' hound you lope along: your bone
  is charmed, and as heavy in the head as stone.

INTRODUCTION

Greeks have been saying no since at least October 28th, 1940. So-called "Ochi Day" (*ochi* means "no" in Modern Greek) commemorates Greek Prime Minister Ioannis Metaxas's refusal to accept terms of capitulation tendered by Mussolini and the Axis powers at the onset of World War II. So momentous was that refusal in the Greek psyche that the day is now celebrated as the national holiday of Greek independence. But in fact, Greeks have been saying no for much longer than that. Achilles declined to fight Trojans for the benefit of an inferior commanding officer. ("The Trojans never did nothin' to me," he effectively tells Agamemnon in the *Iliad*.[1]) The Athenians and their allies said a resounding no to the invading Persians, first in their victory at Marathon in 490 BCE, then again at Salamis ten years later. And then there's Socrates, who refused to live any other life than one dedicated to finding out the truth since, as he put it,

"the unexamined life is not worth living."[2] His fellow citizens executed him regardless.

Diogenes of Sinope, the founder of Cynicism, stands in this tradition of naysaying. That would be a very neat and tidy way of introducing him—if only it were true. But the truth is rather that Diogenes stood outside all traditions. Diogenes pitted a life lived "according to Nature" against one lived in unthinking compliance with Custom. In a sense, every sentence he utters contains a no in it. His nonconformity to convention is nicely epitomized in this anecdote: "'Most people go crazy over a finger,' Diogenes used to say. 'If you walk around with your middle finger extended, a person will think you're nuts, but if you use your forefinger, it's no problem!'"[3] Flippin' the bird is perhaps the ultimate negation. It says no with no questions asked and no explanations given, flouting at the same time the triviality of polite norms. Predictably, Diogenes was not shy about using the gesture—for both of those reasons—as in an encounter with the orator Demosthenes presented below.[4]

Diogenes's indecent behavior and rough, out-of-doors living earned him a nickname: the Dog, which is what the Greek word *kuōn*, whence the adjective *kunikos* ("Cynic"), means. Anyone who

has visited modern Athens will have seen or experienced the city's motley assortment of ownerless dogs roaming the streets and alleyways, pawing through garbage bins, and lounging in the Mediterranean sun (or porticoed shade) amidst the dilapidated remains of high civilization. That is exactly how we are to picture the ancient Athenians picturing Diogenes. With typical self-effacing irony Diogenes embraced the moniker, casting himself as the city's moral watchdog, barking the truth to passersby and biting back at rogues. I will let the selections in this volume speak for themselves on the further details of these matters and introduce some of the major players and key concepts of this way of life. Suffice it to emphasize here that the Cynics were not scholars or writers.[5] Like a Jesus, or a Socrates, or a Buddha, they were oralists whose memorable utterances and actions were transmitted to posterity by admirers (and detractors). The Cynics were, to put it in contemporary terms, lifestylists and performance artists.[6] It is doubtful whether we can even justly call them philosophers, as they did not organize themselves into a school or formulate a set of systematic doctrines.[7] Their mode of life was a philosophy of doing.

And yet the Cynics did purvey some core values that distinguished them in their own time and, I believe, recommend them to ours. Indeed, I think they speak with some urgency to our current predicaments involving climate change, socioeconomic uncertainty, and psychic malaise. Their "less is more" approach to living anticipates the lifestyle experiments of popular culture moguls like thrifty investment advisor Mr. Money Mustache (aka Peter Adeney)[8] and would-be environmental superhero No Impact Man (Colin Beavan).[9] Their obsession with decluttering and detachment aligns with our aspirational fixation on minimalist, nonmaterialistic transcendence. (Marie Kondo has nothing on the Cynics.) *How to Do Nothing*, subtitled *Resisting the Attention Economy*, a best-selling manifesto by Jenny Odell published in 2020, is an art form the Cynics had already perfected back in the 350s—*BCE*.[10]

At a larger scale, the Cynic ethos of "put up and make do" anticipates the modern notion of appropriate technology and its application in contexts where resources are scarce (which is, in our age of extraction and depletion, all contexts).[11] Their disentanglement of needs from wants provides an object lesson in prioritizing human goods. The Cyn-

ics also exemplified the idea that subsistence life-styles are sustainable lifestyles, and the principle behind their lived example gives the lie to the modern article of faith that economic development and growth are synonymous with quality of life. In fact, the Cynics are gurus of degrowth. Finally, their embrace of cosmopolitanism—the Cynics coined the word[12]—flies in the face of the resurgent nativism that threatens the stability of nations, including our own. In *Cosmopolitanism: Ethics in a World of Strangers* (W. W. Norton, 2007) Anthony Appiah takes up the question of how, in today's pluralist world, ethical universals could ever bind people together given that we contend with so many competing particulars. His answer, that they can, and that those universals are rooted in our shared contingency as human beings stripped of all cultural accretions, however impressive and formative of identity those achievements might be (the Parthenon, for example, the Hajj, Angkor Wat, the Bill of Rights, the Internet), was adumbrated by the Cynics.

The Cynics championed their positions on the grounds that their views accorded with states of affairs found in Nature. Their appeal to the example of nonhuman agents, animals in particular, is highly

instructive as it validates the intrinsic worth of the nonhuman world more broadly, foreshadowing thereby a central tenet of modern environmental philosophy. I should be quick to add, though, that it is not so much Cynic *practice* that is exemplary, as entertaining as the sordid details of that may be.[13] Rather, what translates best to our world is the Cynic *mentalité*.

How to Say No contains a mixture of street sermons and verbal repartee, biographical homage and snapshots of Cynics in action. In addition to works by recognized *litterateurs* this brief anthology includes examples of what were probably school exercises where the assignment was to reimagine Cynic escapades and stunts or to explore Cynic psychology through epistolary impersonation. It also celebrates the stubborn persistence of Cynic ideals in early Christian monasticism. Ultimately, the book aims to paint a landscape portrait of ancient Cynicism that aspires to capture the essential features of the terrain—with assorted dogs lazing in the foreground.

But the larger vista remains to be seen: What will you and I say no to? Screen time? Empty relationships? Laziness? Pride? Prejudice? Privilege? Manipulation? Self-centeredness? Dishonesty?

Ambition? Violence? Indulgence? Waste? Greed? Indeed, *cynicism*? This last item in the list shows how far we've fallen. The original Cynics were not cynical in the modern sense. They were ironists, yes, but also realists, who saw human vanities for what they are. Because they sought actively to improve their deficiencies, one might say they were optimists, which is a good note to end on, or, rather, begin with.

But first a final word of thanks is due—to colleagues and friends at the Institute for Advanced Study at Aix-Marseille University and to RFIEA (the French Network of Institutes for Advanced Studies) for a year-long residency in 2021–2022.[14] I'm indebted as well to the University of Vermont for granting a research leave that enabled me to accept the fellowship. Diogenes would not have cared a whit about such honorific privilege, but for my part I am grateful for an opportunity that helped make writing this book possible.

HOW TO SAY NO

1. Life Is a Dog
(Selections from Diogenes Laertius, *Lives and Opinions of Eminent Philosophers*, Book 6)

Diogenes of Sinope (c. 412–323 BCE) is the figurehead of Cynicism, yet almost nothing he is reported to have said or done can be verified with complete certainty. Most of what we hear, however, is likely to be generally *true or as good as true in the sense that Diogenes spawned a movement, and with it a legend, and attracted the attention of many imitators throughout the course of antiquity.*

Diogenes's characteristic schtick is called the chreia, *a short witticism thought to be "useful" (*chrē-simos*) for seasoning one's discourse or for enlarging one's perspective on human folly. Writing* chreiai *attributed to historical persons eventually became a school exercise, which contributes to some of the difficulty in knowing what Diogenes really did or said.*

The following compilation is a Greatest Hits album of Diogenes's antics and bon mots, *plus a few lesser-known B-Sides, drawn from Diogenes Laertius (fl. 3rd century CE), an important source for the history of early Greek philosophy. The Cynic founder's caustic wit, austere lifestyle, yet quiet, serious integrity are on full display here.*

Διογένης Ἱκεσίου τραπεζίτου Σινωπεύς. φησὶ δὲ
Διοκλῆς, δημοσίαν αὐτοῦ τὴν τράπεζαν ἔχοντος τοῦ
πατρὸς καὶ παραχαράξαντος τὸ νόμισμα, φυγεῖν.
Εὐβουλίδης δ' ἐν τῷ Περὶ Διογένους αὐτόν φησι
Διογένην τοῦτο πρᾶξαι καὶ συναλᾶσθαι τῷ πατρί.
οὐ μὴν ἀλλὰ καὶ αὐτὸς περὶ αὐτοῦ φησιν ἐν τῷ
Πορδάλῳ ὡς παραχαράξαι τὸ νόμισμα. ἔνιοι δ'
ἐπιμελητὴν γενόμενον ἀναπεισθῆναι ὑπὸ τῶν τε-
χνιτῶν καὶ ἐλθόντα εἰς Δελφοὺς ἢ εἰς τὸ Δήλιον ἐν
τῇ πατρίδι Ἀπόλλωνος πυνθάνεσθαι εἰ ταῦτα πρά-
ξει ἅπερ ἀναπείθεται· τοῦ δὲ συγχωρήσαντος τὸ πολιτικὸν νόμισμα, οὐ συνείς, τὸ κέρμα ἐκιβδήλευσε καὶ
φωραθείς, ὡς μέν τινες, ἐφυγαδεύθη, ὡς δέ τινες,
ἑκὼν ὑπεξῆλθε φοβηθείς. ἔνιοι δέ φασι παρὰ τοῦ
πατρὸς αὐτὸν λαβόντα τὸ νόμισμα διαφθεῖραι· καὶ
τὸν μὲν δεθέντα ἀποθανεῖν, τὸν δὲ φυγεῖν ἐλθεῖν τ'
εἰς Δελφοὺς καὶ πυνθανόμενον οὐκ εἰ παραχαράξει,
ἀλλὰ τί ποιήσας ἐνδοξότατος ἔσται, οὕτω λαβεῖν
τὸν χρησμὸν τοῦτον.

Exile and Conversion to Philosophy (§§20–22)

Diogenes, the son of Hicesius, a banker, hailed from Sinope. Diocles[1] says that Diogenes was exiled because his father, the man in charge of the public bank, defaced the currency, though Euboulides[2] asserts that it was Diogenes who did this and that his father joined him in exile. Indeed, in the *Pordalus*[3] Diogenes says exactly this in the first person, that he himself defaced the currency. Some also say that while he was acting as overseer he was persuaded by the workers to undertake the deed and traveled either to Delphi or to the Delian Oracle of Apollo in his home country to inquire if he should do what was being asked of him. When the god assented to defacing the *political* currency, Diogenes, not grasping what he meant, adulterated the coinage. When he was found out, he was banished, according to some, while others say he left of his own accord out of fear. Still others say Diogenes took over the currency exchange from his father and engaged in counterfeiting, whereupon his father was imprisoned and died, while Diogenes was exiled,

Γενόμενος δὲ Ἀθήνησιν Ἀντισθένει παρέβαλε. τοῦ δὲ διωθουμένου διὰ τὸ μηδένα προσίεσθαι, ἐξεβιάζετο τῇ προσεδρίᾳ. καί ποτε τὴν βακτηρίαν ἐπανατειναμένου αὐτῷ τὴν κεφαλὴν ὑποσχών, "παῖε," εἶπεν· "οὐ γὰρ εὑρήσεις οὕτω σκληρὸν ξύλον ᾧ με ἀπείρξεις ἕως ἄν τι φαίνῃ λέγων." τοὐντεῦθεν διήκουσεν αὐτοῦ καὶ ἅτε φυγὰς ὢν ὥρμησεν ἐπὶ τὸν εὐτελῆ βίον.

Μῦν θεασάμενος διατρέχοντα . . . καὶ μήτε κοίτην ἐπιζητοῦντα μήτε σκότος εὐλαβούμενον ἢ ποθοῦντά τι τῶν δοκούντων ἀπολαυστῶν, πόρον ἐξεῦρε τῆς περιστάσεως.

Διττὴν δ' ἔλεγεν εἶναι τὴν ἄσκησιν, τὴν μὲν ψυχικήν, τὴν δὲ σωματικήν· ταύτην καθ' ἣν ἐν γυμνασίᾳ συνεχεῖ γινόμεναι φαντασίαι εὐλυσίαν πρὸς τὰ τῆς ἀρετῆς ἔργα παρέχονται. εἶναι δ' ἀτελῆ τὴν

made the trip to Delphi, and inquired not if he should deface the currency, but rather what he could do to become famous and that's how he received the oracle.

On arriving in Athens, he importuned Antisthenes. When Antisthenes rebuffed him, on the grounds that he wasn't accepting students, Diogenes wore him down by pestering. On one occasion, when Antisthenes raised his walking stick at him, Diogenes bowed his head and said, "Strike! You won't find any wood so hard as to keep me away so long as I think you've got something to say." From that point on he became Antisthenes's disciple and, since he was an exile, he embarked upon a life of simplicity.

It was by watching a mouse scurrying about—not anxious for a place to sleep, not afraid of the dark, nor pining away for any of the so-called pleasures—that he discovered the resourcefulness needed to handle tough situations.

Summary of Beliefs (§§70–73 and 103–105)

He used to say that training is twofold, one kind mental, the other physical. Physical training requires constant exercise and enables mental impressions to pass through the system easily with a view to

ἑτέραν χωρὶς τῆς ἑτέρας, οὐδὲν ἧττον εὐεξίας καὶ
ἰσχύος ἐν τοῖς προσήκουσι γενομένης, ὡς περὶ τὴν
ψυχὴν καὶ περὶ τὸ σῶμα. παρετίθετο δὲ τεκμήρια
τοῦ ῥᾳδίως ἀπὸ τῆς γυμνασίας ἐν τῇ ἀρετῇ καταγί-
νεσθαι· ὁρᾶν τε γὰρ ἔν τε ταῖς τέχναις ταῖς βαναύ-
σοις καὶ ταῖς ἄλλαις οὐ τὴν τυχοῦσαν ὀξυχειρίαν
τοὺς τεχνίτας ἀπὸ τῆς μελέτης περιπεποιημένους
τούς τ᾽ αὐλητὰς καὶ τοὺς ἀθλητὰς ὅσον ὑπερφέρου-
σιν ἑκάτεροι τῇ ἰδίᾳ πονήσει τῇ συνεχεῖ, καὶ ὡς
οὗτοι εἰ μετήνεγκαν τὴν ἄσκησιν καὶ ἐπὶ τὴν ψυχήν,
οὐκ ἂν ἀνωφελῶς καὶ ἀτελῶς ἐμόχθουν.

Οὐδέν γε μὴν ἔλεγε τὸ παράπαν ἐν τῷ βίῳ χωρὶς
ἀσκήσεως κατορθοῦσθαι, δυνατὴν δὲ ταύτην πᾶν
ἐκνικῆσαι. δέον οὖν ἀντὶ τῶν ἀχρήστων πόνων τοὺς
κατὰ φύσιν ἑλομένους ζῆν εὐδαιμόνως, παρὰ τὴν
ἄνοιαν κακοδαιμονοῦσι. καὶ γὰρ αὐτὴ τῆς ἡδονῆς ἡ
καταφρόνησις ἡδυτάτη προμελετηθεῖσα, καὶ ὥσπερ
οἱ συνεθισθέντες ἡδέως ζῆν, ἀηδῶς ἐπὶ τοὐναντίον
μετίασιν, οὕτως οἱ τοὐναντίον ἀσκηθέντες ἥδιον
αὐτῶν τῶν ἡδονῶν καταφρονοῦσι. τοιαῦτα διελέ-
γετο καὶ ποιῶν ἐφαίνετο, ὄντως νόμισμα παρα-
χαράττων, μηδὲν οὕτω τοῖς κατὰ νόμον ὡς τοῖς κατὰ
φύσιν διδούς· τὸν αὐτὸν χαρακτῆρα τοῦ βίου
λέγων διεξάγειν ὅνπερ καὶ Ἡρακλῆς, μηδὲν ἐλευ-
θερίας προκρίνων.

performing virtuous deeds. The one kind of training is incomplete without the other, since good conditioning and strength form no less a part of matters that concern us, whether they involve the mind or the body. He would offer proof that abiding in virtue is easy through exercise, for in manual work and other arts craftsmen acquire extraordinary precision in the work of their hands through practice. Shawm players[4] and athletes, too, excel in their craft owing to constant, personal effort. If these individuals were similarly to shift their training to the mind, their efforts would not be ineffectual or without benefit.

Nothing whatsoever in life, he used to say, comes out right without training, and yet training can conquer everything. Accordingly, although those who make choices in accordance with Nature (instead of pursuing fruitless toils) necessarily live a happy life, people persist in stupid misery. For even the despising of pleasure is itself most pleasant once it's become a habit. And just as those who've gotten accustomed to a pleasant life become miserable when they pass over to the opposite state of affairs, so those persons whose training has been the opposite of theirs enjoy despising pleasures with more pleasure than the pleasures themselves.

προσυπογράψομεν δὲ καὶ τὰ κοινῇ ἀρέσκοντα αὐτοῖς, αἵρεσιν καὶ ταύτην εἶναι ἐγκρίνοντες τὴν φιλοσοφίαν, οὐ, καθά φασί τινες, ἔνστασιν βίου. ἀρέσκει οὖν αὐτοῖς τὸν λογικὸν καὶ τὸν φυσικὸν τόπον περιαιρεῖν . . . μόνῳ δὲ προσέχειν τῷ ἠθικῷ. καὶ ὅπερ τινὲς ἐπὶ Σωκράτους, τοῦτο Διοκλῆς ἐπὶ Διογένους ἀναγράφει, τοῦτον φάσκων λέγειν, Δεῖ ζητεῖν

ὅττι τοι ἐν μεγάροισι κακόν τ' ἀγαθόν τε τέτυκται.

παραιτοῦνται δὲ καὶ τὰ ἐγκύκλια μαθήματα . . . περιαιροῦσι δὲ καὶ γεωμετρίαν καὶ μουσικὴν καὶ πάντα τὰ τοιαῦτα. ὁ γοῦν Διογένης πρὸς τὸν ἐπιδεικνύντα αὐτῷ ὡροσκοπεῖον, "χρήσιμον," ἔφη, "τὸ ἔργον πρὸς τὸ μὴ ὑστερῆσαι δείπνου." πρὸς τὸν ἐπιδεικνύμενον αὐτῷ μουσικὸν ἔφη·

Such was the character of his discourse, and he displayed it in action, too, a true defacer of the currency, granting nothing to practices arising from Custom compared to those in accordance with Nature, declaring that he pursued the same quality of life as did Heracles, preferring nothing to freedom.

We will now sketch out some doctrines the Cynics held in common to convey my belief that this sect, too, is a proper philosophical school and not, as some assert, just a way of life. Their official position is to strip away Logic and Physics and apply themselves to Ethics only. And that quip that some ascribe to Socrates, Diocles says originated with Diogenes, namely that what needs looking into is

Whatever bad or good is fashioned in our halls.[5]

They reject the subjects of general education too . . . doing away with geometry and music and such like. Indeed, when someone showed Diogenes a clock, he pronounced it "A useful device to ensure you're not late for dinner." To someone who was performing music for him he said:

γνώμαις γὰρ ἀνδρῶν εὖ μὲν οἰκοῦνται πόλεις,
εὖ δ᾽ οἶκος, οὐ ψαλμοῖσι καὶ τερετίσμασιν.

Ἀρέσκει δ᾽ αὐτοῖς καὶ τέλος εἶναι τὸ κατ᾽ ἀρετὴν
ζῆν . . . ὁμοίως τοῖς στωικοῖς· ἐπεὶ καὶ κοινωνία τις
ταῖς δύο ταύταις αἱρέσεσίν ἐστιν. ὅθεν καὶ τὸν κυ-
νισμὸν εἰρήκασι σύντομον ἐπ᾽ ἀρετὴν ὁδόν.

Ἀρέσκει δ᾽ αὐτοῖς καὶ λιτῶς βιοῦν, αὐτάρκεσι
χρωμένοις σιτίοις καὶ τρίβωσι μόνοις, πλούτου καὶ
δόξης καὶ εὐγενείας καταφρονοῦσιν. ἔνιοι γοῦν καὶ
βοτάναις καὶ παντάπασιν ὕδατι χρῶνται ψυχρῷ
σκέπαις τε ταῖς τυχούσαις καὶ πίθοις, καθάπερ Διογένης, ὃς ἔφασκε θεῶν μὲν ἴδιον εἶναι μηδενὸς
δεῖσθαι, τῶν δὲ θεοῖς ὁμοίων τὸ ὀλίγων χρῄζειν.

Ἀρέσκει δ᾽ αὐτοῖς καὶ τὴν ἀρετὴν διδακτὴν
εἶναι . . . καὶ ἀναπόβλητον ὑπάρχειν· ἀξιέραστόν τε
τὸν σοφὸν καὶ ἀναμάρτητον καὶ φίλον τῷ ὁμοίῳ,
τύχῃ τε μηδὲν ἐπιτρέπειν. τὰ δὲ μεταξὺ ἀρετῆς καὶ
κακίας ἀδιάφορα λέγουσιν.

It is by human intelligence that cities are
   well-managed,
As is the household, not by the picking and
   plucking of strings.[6]

It's also their position that to live according to
virtue is the end or goal in life, just like the Stoics.
Indeed, there is a certain affinity between these
two schools, because of which it has been said that
Cynicism is a shortcut on the road to virtue.[7]

Another of their doctrines is to live frugally, to
eat food conducive to self-maintenance, to wear
only one cloak, and to despise wealth, reputation,
and noble birth. Some Cynics, at least, are vegetari-
ans, drink only cold water and take cover in whatever shelter presents itself, including large storage
jars, as did Diogenes, who used to say that it is the
gods' business to lack nothing, but for the godlike to need only a little.

They also hold that virtue is teachable and a possession that can't be taken away; that the wise man
deserves love, is blameless and friendly to his ilk;
and that we should leave nothing to Fortune.
Things that fall in between virtue and vice they
reckon as morally indifferent.

6.22–23 τρίβωνα διπλώσας πρῶτος κατά τινας διὰ
τὸ ἀνάγκην ἔχειν καὶ ἐνεύδειν αὐτῷ, πήραν τ᾽
ἐκομίσατο, ἔνθα αὐτῷ τὰ σιτία ἦν, καὶ παντὶ τόπῳ
ἐχρῆτο εἰς πάντα, ἀριστῶν τε καὶ καθεύδων καὶ
διαλεγόμενος. ὅτε καὶ τοὺς Ἀθηναίους ἔφασκε,
δεικνὺς τὴν τοῦ Διὸς στοὰν καὶ τὸ Πομπεῖον, αὐτῷ
κατεσκευακέναι ἐνδιαιτᾶσθαι. βακτηρίᾳ δ᾽ ἐπε-
στηρίζετο ἀσθενήσας· ἔπειτα μέντοι καὶ διὰ παντὸς ἐφόρει, οὐ μὴν ἐν ἄστει, ἀλλὰ καθ᾽ ὁδὸν
αὐτῇ τε καὶ τῇ πήρᾳ . . . ἐπιστείλας δέ τινι οἰκίδιον
αὐτῷ προνοήσασθαι, βραδύνοντος, τὸν ἐν τῷ
Μητρῴῳ πίθον ἔσχεν οἰκίαν . . . καὶ θέρους μὲν ἐπὶ
ψάμμου ζεστῆς ἐκυλινδεῖτο, χειμῶνος δ᾽ ἀνδριά-
ντας κεχιονισμένους περιελάμβανε, πανταχόθεν
ἑαυτὸν συνασκῶν.

6.37 συνελογίζετο δὲ καὶ οὕτως· τῶν θεῶν ἐστι
πάντα· φίλοι δὲ οἱ σοφοὶ τοῖς θεοῖς· κοινὰ δὲ τὰ τῶν
φίλων. πάντ᾽ ἄρα ἐστὶ τῶν σοφῶν.

Diogenes in Action . . .

Diogenes was the first, according to some, to fold his cloak double since he had to sleep in it as well. He also carried a knapsack to store his food. When he had grown weak from age, he took to leaning upon a staff and carried it everywhere thereafter—not in town, but on the road—that and his knapsack.[8] . . . He made use of all places for all purposes—for eating breakfast, for sleeping, and for discussions. Sometimes he would say, pointing to the Stoa of Zeus[9] and the Pompeion,[10] that the Athenians had furnished him with places to live. . . . He had written a letter to someone once asking him to buy him a small house. He got a slow response, so he made the large storage jar in the Metroön[11] his home instead. . . . In summer he would roll around in hot sand. In winter he would hug statues covered in snow, thus subjecting himself to training by every means possible. (§22–23)

This is a syllogism he used to employ:

Everything belongs to the gods.
The wise are the gods' friends.
Friends hold things in common.
Ergo: Everything belongs to the wise. (§37)

6.64 εἰς θέατρον εἰσῄει ἐναντίος τοῖς ἐξιοῦσιν· ἐρωτηθεὶς δὲ διὰ τί, "τοῦτο," ἔφη, "ἐν παντὶ τῷ βίῳ ἐπιτηδεύω ποιεῖν."

6.46 ἐπ᾽ ἀγορᾶς ποτε χειρουργῶν, "εἴθε," ἔφη, "καὶ τὴν κοιλίαν ἦν παρατρίψαντα μὴ πεινῆν." (cf. 6.69 χειρουργῶν τ᾽ ἐν τῷ μέσῳ συνεχές, "εἴθε ἦν," ἔλεγε, "καὶ τὴν κοιλίαν παρατριψάμενον τοῦ λιμοῦ παύσασθαι.")

6.35 ξένων δέ ποτε θεάσασθαι θελόντων Δημοσθένην, τὸν μέσον δάκτυλον ἐκτείνας, "οὗτος ὑμῖν," ἔφη, "ἐστὶν ὁ Ἀθηναίων δημαγωγός."

6.37 Θεασάμενός ποτε παιδίον ταῖς χερσὶ πῖνον ἐξέρριψε τῆς πήρας τὴν κοτύλην, εἰπών, "παιδίον με νενίκηκεν εὐτελείᾳ." ἐξέβαλε δὲ καὶ τὸ τρυβλίον, ὁμοίως παιδίον θεασάμενος, ἐπειδὴ κατέαξε τὸ σκεῦος, τῷ κοίλῳ τοῦ ψωμίου τὴν φακῆν ὑποδεχόμενον.

6.24 συνεχές τε ἔλεγεν εἰς τὸν βίον παρεσκευάσθαι δεῖν λόγον ἢ βρόχον.

6.49 εἰπόντος τινός, "Σινωπεῖς σου φυγὴν κατέγνωσαν," "ἐγὼ δέ γε," εἶπεν, "ἐκείνων μονήν."

6.63 ἐρωτηθεὶς πόθεν εἴη, "κοσμοπολίτης," ἔφη.

He used to enter the theater, walking against the flow of people exiting. When asked why, he replied, "I've been pursuing this course of action my entire life." (§64)

He would often give himself a hand job in the middle of the Agora and say, "If only hunger were relieved by stroking one's stomach!"[12]

On one occasion some foreigners were in town and wanted to see the orator Demosthenes. Diogenes pointed him out with his middle finger and said, "There you go—the demagogue of Athens!" (§65)

Once, after observing a child drink water from his hands, he hurled his cup from his knapsack, saying "A child has vanquished me in simplicity!" He tossed out his bowl, too, when he saw in like manner a child who had broken his plate take his lentils in a hollowed-out hunk of bread. (§37)

He was constantly saying that with respect to living life one must either use one's noodle or a noose.[13] (§24)

When someone observed, "The Sinopeans have condemned you to exile," he replied, "Yes, but I have condemned them to stay put." (§49)

When asked where he was from, he replied, "I am a Cosmopolite."[14] (§63)

6.40 πρὸς τὸν πυθόμενον ποίᾳ ὥρᾳ δεῖ ἀριστᾶν, "εἰ μὲν πλούσιος," ἔφη, "ὅταν θέλῃ· εἰ δὲ πένης, ὅταν ἔχῃ."

6.54 ἐρωτηθεὶς ποῖον οἶνον ἡδέως πίνει, ἔφη, "τὸν ἀλλότριον."

6.56 ἐρωτηθεὶς διὰ τί προσαίταις μὲν ἐπιδιδόασι, φιλοσόφοις δὲ οὔ, ἔφη, "ὅτι χωλοὶ μὲν καὶ τυφλοὶ γενέσθαι ἐλπίζουσι, φιλοσοφῆσαι δ' οὐδέποτε."

6.49 ᾔτει ποτὲ ἀνδριάντα· ἐρωτηθεὶς δὲ διὰ τί τοῦτο ποιεῖ, "μελετῶ," εἶπεν, "ἀποτυγχάνειν."

6.41 λύχνον μεθ' ἡμέραν ἅψας περιῄει λέγων "ἄνθρωπον ζητῶ."

6.58 πρὸς τὸν εἰπόντα, "οἱ πλείους σου κατα-γελῶσι," "κἀκείνων τυχόν," εἶπεν, "οἱ ὄνοι· ἀλλ' οὔτ' ἐκεῖνοι τῶν ὄνων ἐπιστρέφονται, οὔτ' ἐγὼ ἐκείνων."

6.60 ἐρωτηθεὶς τί ποιῶν κύων καλεῖται, ἔφη, "τοὺς μὲν διδόντας σαίνων, τοὺς δὲ μὴ διδόντας ὑλακτῶν, τοὺς δὲ πονηροὺς δάκνων."

6.46 ἐν δείπνῳ προσερρίπτουν αὐτῷ τινες ὀστάρια ὡς κυνί· καὶ ὃς ἀπαλλαττόμενος προσεούρησεν αὐτοῖς ὡς κύων.

To someone who asked at what hour one should eat lunch he said, "If rich, whenever you want; if poor, whenever you can." (§40)

When asked what kind of wine he enjoyed drinking, he replied, "Somebody else's." (§54)

When he was asked why people give to beggars but not to philosophers, he said, "Because people expect they might become lame or blind, but never that they'll become philosophers!" (§56)

He once begged from a statue. When asked why he was doing so, he replied, "To get practice at being refused." (§49)

It was his custom to light a lamp in the middle of the day, walk around with it and say, "I'm looking for a human being." (§41)

To someone who said, "Most people laugh at you," he replied, "And, probably, asses laugh at them. People pay no heed to asses. I pay no heed to them." (§58)

When asked what it was that he did to be called a dog, he said, "Because I fawn on those who give, I bark at those who don't, and I bite scoundrels." (§60)

At a dinner party people kept tossing him bones as one would do to a dog, whereupon, like a dog, he pissed on them and left. (§46)

6.54 Ἐρωτηθεὶς ὑπό τινος, "ποῖός τίς σοι Διογένης δοκεῖ;" "Σωκράτης," εἶπε, "μαινόμενος."

6.69 Ἐρωτηθεὶς τί κάλλιστον ἐν ἀνθρώποις, ἔφη, "παρρησία."

6.60 Ἀλεξάνδρου ποτὲ ἐπιστάντος αὐτῷ καὶ εἰπόντος, "ἐγώ εἰμι Ἀλέξανδρος ὁ μέγας βασιλεύς," "κἀγώ," φησί, "Διογένης ὁ κύων."

6.38 ἐν τῷ Κρανείῳ ἡλιουμένῳ αὐτῷ Ἀλέξανδρος ἐπιστάς φησιν, "αἴτησόν με ὃ θέλεις." καὶ ὅς, "ἀποσκότησόν μου," φησί.

6.40 Πλάτωνος ὁρισαμένου, Ἄνθρωπός ἐστι ζῷον δίπουν ἄπτερον, καὶ εὐδοκιμοῦντος, τίλας ἀλεκτρυόνα εἰσήνεγκεν αὐτὸν εἰς τὴν σχολὴν καί φησιν, "οὗτός ἐστιν ὁ Πλάτωνος ἄνθρωπος." ὅθεν τῷ ὅρῳ προσετέθη τὸ πλατυώνυχον.

6.74 Καὶ πρᾶσιν ἤνεγκε γενναιότατα· πλέων γὰρ εἰς Αἴγιναν καὶ πειραταῖς ἁλοὺς ὧν ἦρχε Σκίρπαλος, εἰς Κρήτην ἀπαχθεὶς ἐπιπράσκετο· καὶ τοῦ κήρυκος ἐρωτῶντος τί οἶδε ποιεῖν, ἔφη, "ἀνθρώπων ἄρχειν." ὅτε καὶ δείξας τινὰ Κορίνθιον εὐπάρυφον, τὸν προειρημένον Ξενιάδην, ἔφη, "τούτῳ με πώλει· οὗτος δεσπότου χρῄζει." ὠνεῖται δὴ αὐτὸν ὁ Ξενιάδης καὶ ἀπαγαγὼν εἰς τὴν Κόρινθον ἐπέστησε

When someone asked Plato,[15] "What sort of person does Diogenes seem to you?" he replied, "Socrates gone insane." (§54)

When asked "What is the finest possession of humankind?" he replied, "To speak frankly." (§69)

Alexander once stood before him and declared, "I am Alexander, the Great King." "And I," he replied, "am Diogenes the Dog." (§60)

While Diogenes was sunbathing in the Craneum,[16] Alexander stood in front of him and said, "Ask me for whatever you want," to which Diogenes replied, "Get out of my sunshine." (§38)

While Plato was receiving accolades for defining a human being as a featherless biped, Diogenes plucked a chicken, brought it into the lecture hall and said, "Behold, Plato's human." Whereupon Plato added "flat-fingernailed" to his definition. (§40)

He even bore being sold as a slave with the greatest dignity. For, en route by boat to Aegina, Diogenes was captured by pirates under Scirpalus's command, brought to Crete, and put up for sale. When the auctioneer asked what he knew how to do, he replied, "Rule over people." Then he pointed at a certain Corinthian named Xeniades, who was dressed in fine purple. "Sell me to him," he said.

τοῖς ἑαυτοῦ παιδίοις καὶ πᾶσαν ἐνεχείρισε τὴν οἰκίαν. ὁ δὲ οὕτως αὐτὴν ἐν πᾶσι διετίθει, ὥστε ἐκεῖνος περιιὼν ἔλεγεν· "ἀγαθὸς δαίμων εἰς τὴν οἰκίαν μου εἰσελήλυθε."

Λέγεται δὲ πρὸς τὰ ἐνενήκοντα ἔτη βιοὺς τελευτῆσαι. περὶ δὲ τοῦ θανάτου διάφοροι λέγονται λόγοι· οἱ μὲν γὰρ πολύποδα φαγόντα ὠμὸν χολερικῇ ληφθῆναι καὶ ὧδε τελευτῆσαι· . . . Ἄλλοι φασὶ πολύπουν κυσὶ συμμερίσασθαι βουλόμενον οὕτω δηχθῆναι τοῦ ποδὸς τὸν τένοντα καὶ καταστρέψαι. οἱ μέντοι γνώριμοι αὐτοῦ, καθά φησιν Ἀντισθένης ἐν Διαδοχαῖς, εἴκαζον τὴν τοῦ πνεύματος συγκράτησιν. ἐτύγχανε μὲν γὰρ διάγων ἐν τῷ Κρανείῳ τῷ πρὸ τῆς Κορίνθου γυμνασίῳ· κατὰ δὲ τὸ ἔθος ἧκον οἱ γνώριμοι καὶ αὐτὸν καταλαμβάνουσιν ἐγκεκαλυμμένον καὶ εἴκασαν αὐτὸν κοιμᾶσθαι· οὐδὲ γὰρ ἦν τις νυσταλέος καὶ ὑπνηλός. ὅθεν, ἀποπετάσαντες τὸν τρίβωνα ἔκπνουν αὐτὸν καταλαμβάνουσι καὶ ὑπέλαβον τοῦτο πρᾶξαι βουλόμενον λοιπὸν ὑπεξελθεῖν τοῦ βίου.

Ἔνθα καὶ στάσις, ὥς φασιν, ἐγένετο τῶν γνωρίμων, τίνες αὐτὸν θάψουσιν· ἀλλὰ καὶ μέχρι χει-

"He needs a master." And so Xeniades bought him, took him to Corinth, and put him in charge of his children and all his household. Diogenes managed everything so well that Xeniades went around saying, "A good spirit has entered my home." (§74)

Death (§§76–78)

They say that Diogenes was nearly ninety when he died. Accounts differ as to the manner of his death. Some say he was taken ill after eating raw octopus and that's how he died. . . . Others say that in attempting to share the octopus with dogs he was bitten on the tendon of his foot and succumbed to that. Those who knew him, however, as Antisthenes says in his work *The Successions*, reckon it likely that he died from holding his breath. For he happened to be living in the Craneum, a place for exercise just outside Corinth, and his acquaintances came, as usual, and found him all wrapped up and guessed that he was sleeping. But because he was not, they inferred, the drowsy type, nor prone to nodding off, they peeled back his cloak, found that he wasn't breathing, and supposed he had done the deed on purpose to escape the remainder of his life.

Thereupon an argument arose among his companions about who should bury him. Indeed, they

ρῶν ἦλθον. ἀφικομένων δὲ τῶν πατέρων καὶ τῶν ὑπερεχόντων, ὑπὸ τούτοις ταφῆναι τὸν ἄνδρα παρὰ τῇ πύλῃ τῇ φερούσῃ εἰς τὸν Ἰσθμόν. ἐπέστησάν τ᾽ αὐτῷ κίονα καὶ ἐπ᾽ αὐτῷ λίθου Παρίου κύνα. ὕστερον δὲ καὶ οἱ πολῖται αὐτοῦ χαλκαῖς εἰκόσιν ἐτίμησαν αὐτὸν καὶ ἐπέγραψαν οὕτω·

γηράσκει καὶ χαλκὸς ὑπὸ χρόνου, ἀλλὰ σὸν οὔτι
   κῦδος ὁ πᾶς αἰών, Διόγενες, καθελεῖ·
μοῦνος ἐπεὶ βιοτᾶς αὐτάρκεα δόξαν ἔδειξας
   θνατοῖς καὶ ζωᾶς οἶμον ἐλαφροτάταν.

Ἔνιοι δέ φασι τελευτῶντα αὐτὸν [καὶ] ἐντείλασθαι ἄταφον ῥῖψαι ὡς πᾶν θηρίον αὐτοῦ μετάσχοι, ἢ εἴς γε βόθρον συνῶσαι καὶ ὀλίγην κόνιν ἐπαμῆσαι· οἱ δέ, εἰς τὸν Ἰλισσὸν ἐμβαλεῖν, ἵνα τοῖς ἀδελφοῖς χρήσιμος γένηται.

came to blows over it. But their fathers and leading citizens arrived on the scene and, with their intervention, Diogenes was buried beside the gate that leads to the Isthmus. They erected a column over his grave and placed upon it a dog sculpted in Parian marble. Later his fellow citizens also honored him with statues of bronze, on which they inscribed the following:

Diogenes—
Bronze grows gray with time, but your renown
No eternity can topple down.
You alone showed us, who mortals be,
Life's easiest road and autarky.[17]

But others say his dying wish was to be chucked aside, unburied, so that wild animals could partake of him, or pushed into a ditch at least, with a little dust sprinkled on top; still others that he wanted to be thrown into the river Ilissus so that he might be of some use to his brethren.

2. How Not to Say No

(Seneca, *Letters* 5.1–6)

Seneca (4 BCE–65 CE) was a Stoic, but eclectic in his philosophical taste. He quotes liberally, for example, from Epicurus and showers praise on Demetrius the Cynic, as in selection no. 4 below. Here he offers some sage advice to his friend Lucilius on the theme "nothing in excess" as it pertains to a philosopher's appearance and demeanor. Seneca is critical of ascetic ostentation when it becomes so excessive as to put people off from philosophy altogether. While Cynicism is not named, it is unmistakably described. Seneca recommends instead that we internalize philosophical principles that foster true virtue. His ironic closing remarks highlight the indifference we should feel toward all externals, especially material possessions.

Seneca Lucilio suo salutem:

Quod pertinaciter studes et omnibus omissis hoc unum agis, ut te meliorem cotidie facias, et probo et gaudeo, nec tantum hortor, ut persevere, sed etiam rogo. Illud autem te admoneo, ne eorum more, qui non proficere sed conspici cupiunt, facias aliqua, quae in habitu tuo aut genere vitae notabilia sint. Asperum cultum et intonsum caput et neglegentiorem barbam et indictum argento odium et cubile humi positum, et quicquid aliud ambitio nempe perversa via sequitur, evita. Satis ipsum nomen philosophiae, etiam si modeste tractetur, invidiosum est; quid si nos hominum consuetudini coeperimus excerpere? Intus omnia dissimilia sint, frons populo nostra conveniat. Non splendeat toga, ne sordeat quidem. Non habeamus argentum, in quod solidi auri caelatura descenderit, sed non putemus frugalitatis indicium auro argentoque caruisse. Id agamus, ut meliorem vitam sequamur quam vulgus, non ut contrariam; alioquin quos emendari volumus, fugamus a nobis et avertimus. Illud quoque efficimus, ut nihil imitari velint nostri, dum timent, ne imitanda sint omnia.

Hoc primum philosophia promittit, sensum communem, humanitatem et congregationem. A qua professione dissimilitudo nos separabit. Videamus, ne ista, per quae admirationem parare volumus,

Seneca, to his friend Lucilius, greetings:

I applaud you and rejoice that in your tenacious pursuit of knowledge you put all else aside and focus on this one thing: to make yourself a better person each day. I not only encourage you to continue in this, I demand it. I urge you, however, not to engage in behaviors or a lifestyle in order to stand out, as do those whose desire is not to make moral progress in life but to be noticed. A rough appearance, unkempt hair, a messy beard, a professed hatred for money, a bed strewn on the ground and whatever else self-promotion pursues on its crooked course—avoid these things. The label "philosophy" itself is despised enough already, even if one wears it modestly. What would happen if we began to set ourselves apart from basic human customs? Let everything be different on the *inside*; let our facades agree with everyone else's. Don't make your toga gleam; but don't let it be dirty either. Let us not possess silver plate inlaid with decorations of solid gold; but we shouldn't think that to lack silver and gold is proof of frugality either. Let's be sure we lead a life that's *better* than the average, not contrary to it. Otherwise, we'll scare off those whom we wish to change and they'll turn away from us. Another

ridicula et odiosa sint. Nempe propositum nostrum est secundum naturam vivere; hoc contra naturam est, torquere corpus suum et faciles odisse munditias et squalorem adpetere et cibis non tantum vilibus uti sed taetris et horridis. Quemadmodum desiderare delicatas res luxuriae est, ita usitatas et non magno parabiles fugere dementiae. Frugalitatem exigit philosophia, non poenam, potest autem esse non incompta frugalitas. Hic mihi modus placet: temperetur vita inter bonos mores et publicos; suspiciant omnes vitam nostram, sed agnoscant.

consequence of this kind of behavior is that people will not be keen to imitate anything we do for fear they'll have to imitate all of it. This first and foremost is what philosophy has to offer: a shared sense of purpose, a feeling of belonging to the human race, and coming together in community. Striving to be different cuts us off from that creed. Let's make a point not to make those qualities for which we want to be admired appear laughable or repulsive. Yes, our teaching is in fact to live according to Nature. But to torture one's own body, to despise basic cleanliness, to seek squalor and eat food that is not only vile, but putrid and disgusting is contrary to Nature. Just as it is indicative of luxury to crave dainties, so, too, is it a sign of madness to shun ordinary things that do not cost a lot to come by. The philosophical life demands frugality, not punishment, and a frugality that is not disheveled. This Middle Way suits me: Let our lifestyles observe a mean between good character and public *mores*. Let everyone notice our way of life, but let's be sure they can comprehend it, too.

"Quid ergo? Eadem faciemus, quae ceteri? Nihil inter nos et illos intererit?" Plurimum. Dissimiles esse nos vulgo sciat, qui inspexerit propius. Qui domum intraverit, nos potius miretur quam supellectilem nostram. Magnus ille est, qui fictilibus sic utitur quemadmodum argento. Nec ille minor est, qui sic argento utitur quemadmodum fictilibus. Infirmi animi est pati non posse divitias. . . .

"What, then? Should we behave like everyone else? Shall there be no difference between us and them?" Very much so. Whoever looks closely will see that we are unlike the mob. If someone enters our house, let him admire *us* more than our furniture. It's a great person who uses earthenware as if it were silver plate. And no less great is someone who uses silver as if it were earthenware. It is a sign of a weak mind not to be able to endure riches. . . .

3. Cynic in Swaddling Clothes

(*Cynic Epistles* No. 33, Crates, to Hipparchia)

Hipparchia of Maroneia is the only female Cynic of whom we have any knowledge. Despite an aristocratic upbringing, Hipparchia followed, then fell in love with, Crates of Thebes (365–285 BCE), a disciple of Diogenes, married him, and the two pursued the Cynic life together (Diogenes Laertius 6.7). Performing their conjugal duties in the street proved quite an attraction to passersby (Cornelius Nepos, frag. 14).

This charming, fictitious letter probably originated as a school exercise. In it Crates commends Hipparchia's Cynic fortitude in giving birth and prescribes appropriate Cynic training for their new baby. Citing Crates and Hipparchia's example, the Stoic Epictetus (50–135 CE) admits that Cynic parenthood is possible but concludes that the solitary Cynic is the "true" parent in that his/her concern is for the care of all humanity (Discourses 3.22.67–82). In Cynic Epistle 47 (Diogenes, to Zeno) it is argued, with characteristic cheek, that the prospects of human extinction by not begetting children through marriage would be no more lamentable than the annihilation of wasps or flies.

Ἐπυθόμην σε ἀποτεκεῖν καὶ εὐμαρῶς· σὺ μὲν γὰρ
οὐδὲν ἡμῖν ἐδήλωσας. χάρις δὲ θεῷ καὶ σοί. Πέπεισαι
ἄρα ὅτι τὸ πονεῖν αἴτιόν ἐστι τοῦ μὴ πονεῖν· οὐδὲ γὰρ
ἂν ὧδέ γ' εὐμαρῶς ἀπέκτες, εἰ μὴ κύουσα ἐπόνεις
ὥσπερ οἱ ἀγωνισταί. ἀλλ' αἱ πολλαὶ γυναῖκες, ἐπειδὰν
κύωσι, θρύπτονται· ἐπειδὰν δὲ ἀποτέκωσιν, αἷς δ' ἂν
συμβῇ περισωθῆναι, νοσερὰ τὰ βρέφη γεννῶνται.
ἀλλ' ἐπιδείξασα, εἰ ὅπερ ἐχρῆν ἥκειν ἀφῖκται,
μελέτω σοι τούτου τοῦ σκυλακίου ἡμῶν· μελήσει
δέ, ἐὰν ἀσφαλῶς σαυτῇ παραπλησίως ἐπεισέλθεις.
ἔστω οὖν λουτρὸν μὲν ψυχρόν, σπάργανα δὲ τρίβων,
τροφὴ δὲ γάλακτος ὅσον γε μὴ ἐς κόρον, βαυκαλήσεις
δὲ ἐν ὀστρακίῳ χελώνης· τοῦτο γάρ φασι καὶ πρὸς
νοσήματα παιδικὰ διαφέρειν. ἐπειδὰν δὲ ἐς τὸ λαλεῖν
ἢ περιπατεῖν ἔλθῃ, κοσμήσασα αὐτὸ μὴ ξίφει, ὥσπερ
ἡ Αἴθρα τὸν Θησέα, ἀλλὰ βακτηρίᾳ καὶ τρίβωνι καὶ
πήρᾳ, τοῖς μᾶλλον δυναμένοις φυλάττειν ἀνθρώπους
ξιφῶν, πέμπε Ἀθήναζε. τὰ δ' ἄλλα ἡμῖν μελήσει
πελαργὸν ἐς τὸ γῆρας ἑαυτῶν ἀντὶ κυνὸς θρέψαι.

I've just learned you've given birth, and it must have been an easy one, for you've said nothing to me. But thank God—and thank *you*. You are now, I take it, persuaded that to experience hardship is the cause of experiencing no hardship. For you would not have delivered so easily if you hadn't labored hard as athletes do whilst you were pregnant. Most women fall to pieces when they're pregnant, and those who happen to survive childbirth deliver sickly babies. Having shown now what you're made of, since the outcome was exactly as it should have been, take care of this little pup of ours. And you will—if you embark upon his care steadfastly, in a way consistent with who you are. Accordingly, let his bathwater be cold, his swaddling clothes be a cloak, and his food be milk—just enough, not to excess—and rock him to sleep in a tortoise shell. (They say this is excellent for preventing childhood diseases.) And when he begins to walk and talk, fit him out not with a sword as Aethra did Theseus, but with a staff, a cloak, and a knapsack, which can provide better protection against people than swords, and send him to Athens.[1] As for the rest, it'll be our job to raise a stork for our old age instead of a dog![2]

4. My Friend Demetrius

(Seneca, *De Beneficiis* 7.1–2 and 8–11)

The long and sprawling essay from which this passage is lifted concerns the giving and receiving of gifts.[1] In this excerpt Seneca showers praise on Demetrius the Cynic (10–90 CE) for his unpretentious simplicity, frugality, and courage to say no to power. (He was twice exiled from Rome for such outspokenness.) The two mini-sermons presented here, as imagined or remembered by Seneca, epitomize Cynic preaching in the first century CE. Seneca pulls out all the stops to ventriloquize Demetrius's impassioned, but no-nonsense style. (Latin was probably a second language for Greek-speaking Demetrius, who came to Rome from Corinth.) Despite his Cynic ways, Demetrius moved comfortably in elite circles. Seneca, for example, one of the wealthiest men in Rome at the time, considered him a friend, and he seems to have been a confidant and perhaps supporter of the Roman statesman Thrasea Paetus, who was executed for his involvement in a Stoic plot to assassinate Nero. (Seneca, too, was implicated and forced to commit suicide.) As far as we know, Demetrius himself died a natural death at a ripe old age.

Egregie enim hoc dicere Demetrius Cynicus, vir meo iudicio magnus, etiam si maximis comparetur, solet plus prodesse, si pauca praecepta sapientiae teneas, sed illa in promptu tibi et in usu sint, quam si multa quidem didiceris, sed illa non habeas ad manum. "Quemadmodum," inquit, "magnus luctator est, non qui omnes numeros nexusque perdidicit, quorum usus sub adversario rarus est, sed qui in uno se aut altero bene ac diligenter exercuit et eorum occasiones intentus expectat (neque enim refert, quam multa sciat, si scit, quantum victoriae satis est), sic in hoc studio multa delectant, pauca vincunt. . . .

non multum tibi nocebit transisse, quae nec licet scire nec prodest. Involuta Veritas in alto latet. Nec de malignitate naturae queri possumus, quia nullius rei difficilis inventio est, nisi cuius hic unus inventae fructus est invenisse; quidquid nos meliores beatosque facturum est, aut in aperto aut in prox-

Demetrius the Cynic, a great man in my view, even when compared to the greatest, regularly makes this remarkable point: It is more beneficial to hold only a few philosophical views that you have ready to put to good use than to have learned many arguments that you don't keep close to hand. "It's like wrestling," he says. "The great wrestler is not one who has mastered an encyclopedia of grips and holds, the use of which against an adversary is rare. Rather it's the one who's trained himself with care and diligence in one or two maneuvers and waits intently for the right moment to use them. In other words, it doesn't matter how many moves he knows provided he knows how much is enough to win. So, too, in the pursuit of philosophy: many topics bring delight, but only a few confer victory." . . .

"To skip over what you might not know or what is of no use won't hurt you much. 'Truth lies hidden, shrouded, in the depths.'[2] But we cannot complain for that reason that Nature is niggardly, for to discover something is not the problem—unless its only benefit, once discovered, is the fact of its having been discovered. No, Nature has put what

imo posuit. Si animus fortuita contempsit, si se supra metus sustulit nec avida spe infinita complectitur, sed didicit a se petere divitias; si deorum hominumque formidinem eiecit et scit non multum esse ab homine timendum, a deo nihil; si contemptor omnium, quibus torquetur vita, dum ornatur, eo perductus est, ut illi liqueat mortem nullius mali materiam esse, multorum finem; si animum virtuti consecravit et, quacumque vocat illa, planum putat; si sociale animal et in commune genitus mundum ut unam omnium domum spectat et conscientiam suam dis aperuit semperque tamquam in publico vivit se magis veritus quam alios: subductus ille tempestatibus in solido ac sereno stetit consummavitque scientiam utilem ac necessariam. Reliqua oblectamenta otii sunt; licet enim iam in tutum retracto animo ad haec quoque excurrere cultum, non robur, ingeniis adferentia."

will make us better and happier persons in plain view and close by. If your mind has come to spurn chance; if it rises above fear and is not entangled by unbounded hope sprung from greed but has learned to seek its riches from itself; if it has cast off dread of the gods and of people in the knowledge that there's not much to fear from a human being and nothing to fear from a god; if it is full of contempt for all of life's ornaments (which serve also to torture us); if it reaches the point of clarity to see that death is not the source, but the end of many evils; if it consecrates itself to Virtue and thinks that whatever place to which Virtue summons us is a level plain; if, as a social being born for the common good, the mind looks upon the universe as the home for all, lays bare its conscience before the gods and always lives as if it were in full public view, concerned more for self-respect than for what others think—*that* mind, whisked away from the storm-fronts, has come to stand on solid ground under clear skies and has reached the pinnacle of useful and necessary knowledge. Everything else is just amusement for an idle hour. Once the mind has withdrawn to this safe retreat, *then* it may chase after things that bring refinement to one's natural abilities, even if they confer no strength."

Haec Demetrius noster utraque manu tenere proficientem iubet, haec nusquam dimittere, immo adfigere et partem sui facere eoque cotidiana meditatione perduci, ut sua sponte occurrant salutaria et ubique ac statim desiderata praesto sint et sine ulla mora veniat illa turpis honestique distinctio. Sciat nec malum esse ullum nisi turpe nec bonum nisi honestum. Hac regula vitae opera distribuat; ad hanc legem et agat cuncta et exigat miserrimosque mortalium iudicet, in quantiscumque opibus refulgebunt, ventri ac libidini deditos quorumque animus inerti otio torpet. . . .

. . . . . .

Ergo cum animum sapientis intuemur potentem omnium et per universa dimissum, omnia illius esse dicimus, cum ad hoc ius cotidianum, si ita res tulerit, capite censebitur. Multum interest, possessio eius animo ac magnitudine aestimetur an censu. . . .

For those pursuing the good life these are the precepts my friend Demetrius demands we grasp with both hands and never let go of—to cling to them, in fact, to make them part of oneself, and to reach a pitch of mindfulness each day that these sound teachings occur to us of their own accord, so they're handy whenever and wherever they're wanted. That important distinction between what is honest and what is base will also come to us without delay. There is no other bad, mind you, except baseness and no other good besides honesty. Apply this rule across life's work. Act—and exact—in every situation according to this law. Judge those whose minds are sluggish from inert inaction, who are given over to the paunch and to pleasure, however resplendent in riches they might be, as the most wretched of human beings. . . .

And so, when we consider the mind of a sage, which has power over all and is free and clear in all respects, we declare that everything belongs to that person, even if, according to everyday law, were he to be assessed financially, he will be classed in the lowest census category. But there's a big difference between estimating one's net worth by the greatness of one's mind and by the census. . . .

Non referam tibi Socraten, Chrysippum, Zenonem et ceteros magnos quidem viros, maiores quidem, quia in laudem vetustorum invidia non obstat. Paulo ante Demetrium rettuli, quem mihi videtur rerum natura nostris tulisse temporibus, ut ostenderet nec illum a nobis corrumpi nec nos ab illo corripi posse, virum exactae, licet neget ipse, sapientiae firmaeque in iis, quae proposuit, constantiae, eloquentiae vero eius, quae res fortissimas deceat, non concinnatae nec in verba sollicitae, sed ingenti animo, prout impetus tulit, res suas prosequentis. Huic non dubito quin providentia et talem vitam et talem dicendi facultatem dederit, ne aut exemplum saeculo nostro aut convicium deesset.

Demetrio si res nostras aliquis deorum possidendas velit tradere sub lege certa, ne liceat donare, adfirmaverim repudiaturum dicturumque: "Ego vero me ad istud inextricabile pondus non adligo nec in altam faecem rerum hunc expeditum hominem demitto. Quid ad me defers populorum omnium mala? Quae ne daturus quidem acciperem, quoniam multa video, quae me donare non deceat.

I will not invoke for you Socrates, Chrysippus, Zeno and the rest,[3] who are certainly great men, *very* great in fact, since envy does not stand in the way of praise for the ancients. Just moments ago, I invoked Demetrius. It seems to me that Nature has brought him forth in our times to show that he could not be corrupted by us, nor we corrected by him.[4] Demetrius was a man of consummate wisdom, though he himself might disclaim it, and of steadfast consistency in following his own teachings, possessing a kind of eloquence suited to the toughest issues—not pretty, nor bothered about its wording, but appropriate to its subject matter, big-hearted, as his inspiration propelled it. I have no doubt that Providence gave him this kind of life-style and power of speaking so that our age would not lack a model—or a rebuke.

Should some god wish to hand over all our possessions to Demetrius's ownership on the set condition that he not be allowed to give them away, I maintain that he would refuse them saying, "Me? I'm not tying myself to a burden like the one you're offering, one that cannot be untangled. Nor am I, a person free from bonds, sending myself down to the bottom of the barrel. Why assign to me the woes of all humanity? I would not accept such

"Volo sub conspectu meo ponere, quae gentium oculos regumque praestringunt, volo intueri pretia sanguinis animarumque vestrarum. Prima mihi luxuriae spolia propone, sive illa vis per ordinem expandere sive, ut est melius, in unum acervum dare.

"Video elaboratam scrupulosa distinctione testudinem et foedissimorum pigerrimorumque animalium testas ingentibus pretiis emptas, in quibus ipsa illa, quae placet, varietas subditis medicamentis in similitudinem veri coloratur.

"Video istic mensas et aestimatum lignum senatorio censu, eo pretiosius, quo illud in plures nodos arboris infelicitas torsit.

"Video istic crystallina, quorum accendit fragilitas pretium; omnium enim rerum voluptas apud imperitos ipso, quo fugari debet, periculo crescit.

"Video murrea pocula; parum scilicet luxuria magno fuerit, nisi, quod vomant, capacibus gemmis inter se propinaverint.

things even if I were to give them away since I see many things that are not *fit* for me to give away.

"I wish to put in my line of sight those things that blind the eyes of states and kings. I wish to behold the price of your blood and souls. Lay out for me first the spoils of Luxury. Spread them out in a row, please, or even better, dump them into one heap!

"I see tortoises decorated with intricate, distinguishing designs—the shells of that ugliest, slowest of animals purchased at great expense. Yet, the variety of color that pleases us about them in the first place is tinted over with dyes to make them look real!

"I see over there tables made of wood that are valued for as much money as it takes to qualify as a Senator—and the more the unlucky tree happens to have been twisted into knots, the more pricey the table becomes!

"I see here crystal ornaments, whose fragility increases their value. Among the naive the pleasure derived from everything is increased by danger— the very danger that should avert pleasure!

"I see goblets made of murrine:[5] Luxury seems to cost too little unless people can raise a glass of what they will later vomit up using cups studded with huge gems!

"Video uniones non singulos singulis auribus comparatos; iam enim exercitatae aures oneri ferundo sunt; iunguntur inter se et insuper alii binis superponuntur. Non satis muliebris insania viros superiecerat, nisi bina ac terna patrimonia auribus singulis pependissent.

"Video sericas vestes, si vestes vocandae sunt, in quibus nihil est, quo defendi aut corpus aut denique pudor possit, quibus sumptis parum liquido nudam se non esse iurabit. Hae ingenti summa ab ignotis etiam ad commercium gentibus accersuntur, ut matronae nostrae ne adulteris quidem plus sui in cubiculo, quam in publico ostendant.

"Quid agis, avaritia? Quot rerum caritate aurum tuum victum est! Omnia ista, quae rettuli, in maiore honore pretioque sunt. Nunc volo tuas opes

"I see pearls—not single pearls, one fitted to each ear, for these days ears have been trained to bear a heavy load. No, I see pearls fastened together and other pearls placed upon those pairs. Apparently, a woman's madness would not have been enough to bowl men over unless twice or thrice an inheritance hung in each ear.

"I see clothing made from silk—if one can call it clothing, since there's nothing in it by which either one's body or modesty can be protected. When a woman wears such garments, she will be too little transparent to swear she is not naked! These items are procured for a huge sum from peoples unknown to us, unknown even via trade, all so that our wives do not show more of themselves even to their illicit lovers in the bedroom than they do when they're out and about!

"And how are you getting on, Greed? How many things your gold has conquered in its costliness! All those items I was just surveying are held in quite high esteem and fetch a rather high price. Now I wish to review *your* riches: thin slices of two raw materials, which, in order to obtain, our greediness gropes in darkness. And yet, assuredly, the Earth, which brought forth whatever was to be of use to us, buried those things and sunk them deep,

recognoscere, lamnas utriusque materiae, ad quam cupiditas nostra caligat. At mehercules terra, quae, quidquid utile futurum nobis erat, protulit, ista defodit et mersit et ut noxiosis rebus ac malo gentium in medium prodituris toto pondere incubuit. Video ferrum ex isdem tenebris esse prolatum, quibus aurum et argentum, ne aut instrumentum in caedes mutuas deesset aut pretium. Et tamen adhuc ista aliquam materiam habent; est, in quo errorem oculorum animus subsequi possit. Video istic diplomata et syngraphas et cautiones, vacua habendi simulacra, umbracula avaritiae quaedam laborantis, per quae decipiat animum inanium opinione gaudentem. Quid enim ista sunt, quid fenus et calendarium et usura, nisi humanae cupiditatis extra naturam quaesita nomina?

"Possum de rerum natura queri, quod aurum argentumque non interius absconderit, quod non illis maius, quam quod detrahi posset, pondus

and lay upon them with all her weight, thinking them the most harmful substances and a bane to nations if they were to be discovered in plain sight. I observe that iron is mined from the same dark recesses as silver and gold so that we might not lack the instrument—or the payback—for killing one another. Still, *those* materials do nonetheless have actual substance. There is something else by which the mind can be led astray by an optical illusion: I see yonder written certificates, IOUs, and contracts—empty images, devoid of real ownership, the shadowy bowers of Greed as it tries to work out a way to trick empty-headed people whose minds take pleasure in fantasies. But what are these things? What are 'profit,' 'an account book,' and 'interest' other than names made up for human greed that exceeds the bounds of Nature?

"I can complain that Nature didn't stash away her gold and silver more deeply within her, that she did not lay a heavier weight upon them, one that could not be dragged away. But what are these ledgers, these invoices, *time itself* for sale![6] And the blood-sucking ten percent interest a month? They're evils sprung from our choices and our dispositions, that's what they are. There's nothing in them that

iniecerit: quid sunt istae tabellae, quid computatio-
nes et venale tempus et sanguinulentae centesi-
mae? Voluntaria mala ex constitutione nostra pen-
dentia, in quibus nihil est, quod subici oculis, quod
teneri manu possit, inanis avaritiae somnia.

"O miserum, si quem delectate patrimonii sui
liber magnus et vasta spatia terrarum colenda per
vinctos et immensi greges pecorum per provincias
ac regna pascendi et familia bellicosis nationibus
maior et aedificia privata laxitatem urbium mag-
narum vincentia! Cum bene ista, per quae divitias
suas disposuit ac fudit, circumspexerit superbum-
que se fecerit, quidquid habet, ei, quod cupit, com-
paret: pauper est.

"Dimitte me et illis divitiis meis redde. Ego reg-
num sapientiae novi, magnum, securum; ego sic
omnia habeo, ut omnium sint."

can be held in the hand or put before the eyes—
dreams only, of empty Greed!

"If the holdings list of one's own estate is a person's source of pleasure, what wretchedness! So
too, if vast spates of land that must be cultivated by
chain gangs, and huge flocks and herds that must
be pastured on the territory of whole provinces and
kingdoms; if household slaves are more numerous
than the populations of enemy nations, and the size
of private structures outstrips the expansiveness of
great cities—if these are the source of one's pleasure, what wretchedness! When a man has care-
fully taken stock of those things in which he's
invested—and wasted—his wealth and has counted
himself superior for it, let him compare all that he
has with what he still craves, and he is a pauper
nonetheless.

"Send me off now and return me to the riches that
are mine: I am familiar with the kingdom of wisdom, which is magnificent and secure. The way
that *I* own everything results in everything belonging to all."

And so, accordingly, when the Emperor Gaius
Caligula was poised to give Demetrius two hundred
thousand sesterces, he burst out laughing and refused it, as he considered it an amount not even

Itaque cum C. Caesar illi ducenta donaret, ridens reiecit ne dignam quidem summam iudicans, qua non accepta gloriaretur. Di deaeque, quam pusillo animo illum aut honorare voluit aut corrumpere! Reddendum egregio viro testimonium est; ingentem rem ab illo dici audivi, cum miraretur Gai dementiam, quod se putasset tanti posse mutari. "Si temptare," inquit, "me constituerat, toto illi fui experiendus imperio."

worth bragging about having declined. O gods and goddesses, what small thinking stood behind Gaius's intent, regardless of whether it was to honor Demetrius or to corrupt him! I must bear witness to this outstanding man: I heard Demetrius make a powerful comment regarding his amazement at Gaius's madness, that he thought he could be influenced by so great an amount. "If he intended to tempt me," he said, "I should have been tested by an offer of the whole Empire."

5. Student Tribute

(Lucian, *Life of Demonax*, abridged)

In selection no. 3 we saw a schoolboy's attempt to domesticate the Cynics. Lucian's homage to Demonax (70–170 CE), his teacher, runs in a similar vein. Lucian hailed from the Syrian town of Samosata on the fringes of the Roman Empire. Greek was probably his second language after Syriac, but he was nonetheless an arch-Hellene, a voluminous writer, and a wicked satirist. His exposé of Demonax's contemporary, Peregrinus Proteus (95–165 CE), is a merciless indictment of a Christian convert-turned-Cynic imposter. Demonax, however, cuts quite a different figure. He has clearly embraced Cynic trappings and subscribes to Cynic teachings, but is portrayed by Lucian as urbane, sophisticated, and an active participant in his community (Athens). He is, in short, an ideal philosophic type for a litterateur like Lucian himself. The example of Demonax suggests that Cynicism could attract adherents of various backgrounds and temperaments.

Ἔμελλεν ἄρα μηδὲ ὁ καθ᾽ ἡμᾶς βίος τὸ παντάπασιν
ἄμοιρος ἔσεσθαι ἀνδρῶν λόγου καὶ μνήμης ἀξίων,
ἀλλὰ καὶ σώματος ἀρετὴν ὑπερφυᾶ καὶ γνώμην
ἄκρως φιλόσοφον ἐκφαίνειν· λέγω δὲ εἴς τε τὸν
Βοιώτιον Σώστρατον ἀναφέρων, ὃν Ἡρακλέα οἱ
Ἕλληνες ἐκάλουν καὶ ᾤοντο εἶναι, καὶ μάλιστα εἰς
Δημώνακτα τὸν φιλόσοφον, οὓς καὶ εἶδον αὐτὸς καὶ
ἰδὼν ἐθαύμασα, θατέρῳ δὲ τῷ Δημώνακτι καὶ ἐπὶ
μήκιστον συνεγενόμην. περὶ μὲν οὖν Σωστράτου ἐν
ἄλλῳ βιβλίῳ γέγραπταί μοι καὶ δεδήλωται μέγεθός
τε αὐτοῦ καὶ ἰσχύος ὑπερβολὴ καὶ ἡ ὕπαιθρος ἐν τῷ
Παρνασσῷ δίαιτα καὶ ἡ ἐπίπονος εὐνὴ καὶ τροφαὶ
ὄρειοι καὶ ἔργα οὐκ ἀπῳδὰ τοῦ ὀνόματος ὅσα ἢ
λῃστὰς αἴρων ἔπραξεν ἢ ὁδοποιῶν τὰ ἄβατα ἢ γε-
φυρῶν τὰ δύσπορα. περὶ δὲ Δημώνακτος ἤδη δίκαιον
λέγειν ἀμφοῖν ἕνεκα, ὡς ἐκεῖνός τε διὰ μνήμης εἴη
τοῖς ἀρίστοις τό γε κατ᾽ ἐμὲ καὶ οἱ γενναιότατοι τῶν
νέων καὶ πρὸς φιλοσοφίαν ὁρμῶντες ἔχοιεν μὴ πρὸς
τὰ ἀρχαῖα μόνα τῶν παραδειγμάτων σφᾶς αὐτοὺς
ῥυθμίζειν, ἀλλὰ κἀκ τοῦ ἡμετέρου βίου κανόνα προ-
τίθεσαι καὶ ζηλοῦν ἐκεῖνον ἄριστον ὧν οἶδα ἐγὼ φιλοσόφων γενόμενον.

It was, I now see, bound to be the case that our life-time should not be entirely unallotted its share of men worth remembering in writing. Indeed, this age has produced individuals possessing extreme physical prowess and an acutely philosophic mind-set. I speak with reference to Sostratus, a Boeo-tian, whom the Greeks used to call Heracles (and thought was in fact Heracles), and to the philoso-pher Demonax. I myself observed both men in ac-tion and came away amazed at what I saw. With Demonax I spent a considerable amount of time. About Sostratus I have written in another book,[1] where I describe his size and tremendous strength, his living outdoors on Mount Parnassus, his sleep-ing rough, his mountain diet, and the labors he performed in keeping with his nickname as he rounded up and dispensed with thieves, built roads in trackless country, and bridged over difficult passes. But it is right that I should now speak of Demonax, for two reasons. First, so he might be re-membered by persons of influence as far as lies in my power; and second, so that well-intentioned young people eager to pursue philosophy can pat-tern themselves not after ancient models only, but also set themselves a standard drawn from our own

Ἦν δὲ τὸ μὲν γένος Κύπριος, οὐ τῶν ἀφανῶν ὅσα εἰς ἀξίωμα πολιτικὸν καὶ κτῆσιν. οὐ μὴν ἀλλὰ καὶ πάντων τούτων ὑπεράνω γενόμενος καὶ ἀξιώσας ἑαυτὸν τῶν καλλίστων πρὸς φιλοσοφίαν ὥρμησεν οὐκ Ἀγαθοβούλου μὰ Δί᾽ οὐδὲ Δημητρίου πρὸ αὐτοῦ οὐδὲ Ἐπικτήτου ἐπεγειράντων, ἀλλὰ πᾶσι μὲν συνεγένετο τούτοις καὶ ἔτι Τιμοκράτει τῷ Ἡρακλεώτῃ σοφῷ ἀνδρὶ φωνῇ τε καὶ γνώμην μάλιστα κεκοσμημένῳ· ἀλλ᾽ ὅ γε Δημῶναξ οὐχ ὑπὸ τούτων τινός, ὡς ἔφην, παρακληθείς, ἀλλ᾽ ὑπ᾽ οἰκείας πρὸς τὰ καλὰ ὁρμῆς καὶ ἐμφύτου πρὸς φιλοσοφίαν ἔρωτος ἐκ παίδων εὐθὺς κεκινημένος ὑπερεῖδεν μὲν τῶν ἀνθρωπείων ἀγαθῶν ἁπάντων, ὅλον δὲ παραδοὺς ἑαυτὸν ἐλευθερίᾳ καὶ παρρησίᾳ διετέλεσεν αὐτός τε ὀρθῷ καὶ ὑγιεῖ καὶ ἀνεπιλήπτῳ βίῳ χρώμενος καὶ τοῖς ὁρῶσι καὶ ἀκούουσι παράδειγμα παρέχων τὴν ἑαυτοῦ γνώμην καὶ τὴν ἐν τῷ φιλοσοφεῖν ἀλήθειαν. οὐ μὴν ἀνίπτοις γε ποσίν, τὸ τοῦ λόγου, πρὸς ταῦτα ᾖξεν, ἀλλὰ καὶ ποιηταῖς σύντροφος ἐγένετο καὶ τῶν πλείστων ἐμέμνητο καὶ λέγειν ἤσκητο καὶ τὰς ἐν φιλοσοφίᾳ προαιρέσεις οὐκ ἐπ᾽ ὀλίγον

lifetime and emulate that—namely Demonax, the finest philosopher I know.

He was Cypriot by birth, and not undistinguished in terms of his civic stature and the properties he owned. Still, he rose above all that, thinking he was worth the best that life had to offer, and so set out on a philosophic path. It wasn't Agathoboulus or Demetrius before him nor Epictetus who urged him on, though he was associated with all of those teachers and with Timocrates of Heraclea, a wise man especially well endowed with intelligence and a way with words.[2] What I mean is that Demonax did not receive his calling from any of these figures but was prompted even in childhood by a natural inclination toward goodness and by an innate passion for philosophy such that he despised all the things most people count as good and surrendered himself entirely to the pursuit of freedom and frankness in speech. He thus lived a life that was straightforward, healthy, and unassailable, providing a model of right-mindedness and philosophic truth to those who saw and heard him. By no means, though, did he rush into these matters with unwashed feet, as the saying goes. Rather, he was reared on the poets and knew most of them from memory. He was also trained in

οὐδὲ κατὰ τὴν παροιμίαν ἄκρῳ τῷ δακτύλῳ ἁψά-
μενος ἠπίστατο, καὶ τὸ σῶμα δὲ ἐγεγύμναστο καὶ
πρὸς καρτερίαν διεπεπόνητο, καὶ τὸ ὅλον ἐμεμελήκει
αὐτῷ μηδενὸς ἄλλου προσδεᾶ εἶναι· ὥστε ἐπεὶ καὶ
ἔμαθεν οὐκέτι ἑαυτῷ διαρκῶν, ἑκὼν ἀπῆλθε τοῦ
βίου πολὺν ὑπὲρ αὐτοῦ λόγον τοῖς ἀρίστοις τῶν Ἑλλήνων καταλιπών.

Φιλοσοφίας δὲ εἶδος οὐχ ἓν ἀποτεμόμενος, ἀλλὰ
πολλὰς ἐς ταὐτὸ καταμίξας οὐ πάνυ τι ἐξέφαινε τίνι
αὐτῶν ἔχαιρεν· ἐῴκει δὲ τῷ Σωκράτει μᾶλλον
ᾠκειῶσθαι, εἰ καὶ τῷ σχήματι καὶ τῇ τοῦ βίου ῥα-
στώνῃ τὸν Σινωπέα ζηλοῦν ἔδοξεν, οὐ παραχαράτ-
των τὰ εἰς τὴν δίαιταν, ὡς θαυμάζοιτο καὶ ἀποβλέ-
ποιτο ὑπὸ τῶν ἐντυγχανόντων, ἀλλ' ὁμοδίαιτος
ἅπασι καὶ πεζὸς ὢν καὶ οὐδ' ἐπ' ὀλίγον τύφῳ κάτο-
χος συνῆν καὶ ξυνεπολιτεύετο, τὴν μὲν τοῦ Σωκράτους εἰρωνείαν οὐ προσιέμενος, χάριτος δὲ Ἀττι-
κῆς μεστὰς ἀποφαίνων τὰς συνουσίας, ὡς τοὺς

public speaking. Nor did he gain knowledge of the philosophical schools in a short time, or, as the proverb puts it, touching them with just the tip of his finger. Moreover, he had already trained his body and subjected it to hardships to toughen it up. On the whole he had made it his concern not to need anything from anyone else. Accordingly, when he realized that he was no longer self-sufficient, he departed this life on his own terms,[3] leaving behind quite a legacy of himself among well-placed Greeks.

Additionally, he did not carve out for himself one type of philosophy but mixed many kinds into one and would never let on which kind pleased him best. He was likely more at home with Socrates even if he seemed to emulate the man from Sinope in dress and in the carefree manner of his life. He did not deface the currency of everyday life, however, in order to astonish or be noticed by the people he encountered, but lived like everyone else, an ordinary person, totally free from pretense. He even participated in the affairs of the city. But the irony of Socrates was not his style. Rather, his conversations were full of Attic charm, such that the people he mingled with went away without condemning him as boorish or as if they had escaped from depressing criticisms. Instead, they came

προσομιλήσαντας ἀπιέναι μήτε καταφρονήσαντας
ὡς ἀγεννοῦς μήτε τὸ σκυθρωπὸν τῶν ἐπιτιμήσεων
ἀποφεύγοντας, παντοίους δὲ ὑπ᾽ εὐφροσύνης γε-
νομένους καὶ κοσμιωτέρους παρὰ πολὺ καὶ φαι-
δροτέρους καὶ πρὸς τὸ μέλλον εὐέλπιδας. οὐδεπώποτε γοῦν ὤφθη κεκραγὼς ἢ ὑπερδιατεινόμενος ἢ
ἀγανακτῶν, οὐδ᾽ εἰ ἐπιτιμᾶν τῳ δέοι, ἀλλὰ τῶν μὲν
ἁμαρτημάτων καθήπτετο, τοῖς δὲ ἁμαρτάνουσι συ-
νεγίνωσκεν, καὶ τὸ παράδειγμα παρὰ τῶν ἰατρῶν
ἠξίου λαμβάνειν τὰ μὲν νοσήματα ἰωμένων, ὀργῇ
δὲ πρὸς τοὺς νοσοῦντας οὐ χρωμένων· ἡγεῖτο γὰρ
ἀνθρώπου μὲν εἶναι τὸ ἁμαρτάνειν, θεοῦ δὲ ἢ ἀνδρὸς ἰσοθέου τὰ πταισθέντα ἐπανορθοῦν.

Τοιούτῳ δὴ βίῳ χρώμενος εἰς ἑαυτὸν μὲν οὐδενὸς
ἐδεῖτο, φίλοις δὲ συνέπραττε τὰ εἰκότα, καὶ τοὺς μὲν
εὐτυχεῖν δοκοῦντας αὐτῶν ὑπεμίμνησκεν ὡς ἐπ᾽
ὀλιγοχρονίοις τοῖς δοκοῦσιν ἀγαθοῖς ἐπαιρομένους,
τοὺς δὲ ἢ πενίαν ὀδυρομένους ἢ φυγὴν δυσχεραίνο-
ντας ἢ γῆρας ἢ νόσον. αἰτιωμένους σὺν γέλωτι παρε-
μυθεῖτο, οὐχ ὁρῶντας ὅτι μετὰ μικρὸν αὐτοῖς παύσε-
ται μὲν τὰ ἀνιῶντα, λήθη δέ τις ἀγαθῶν καὶ κακῶν καὶ

away variously affected by joy, far more composed, cheerful, and optimistic about the future. You never saw him shouting or agitated or angry, even if he had to upbraid someone, for while he attacked their sins, he forgave the sinners. In this he was of the mind to model himself on the doctors who treat sicknesses but feel no anger toward their patients. He believed that to err is human, but that it was a god's job, or godly man's, to straighten out what has gone awry.

Because he led the life he did, he lacked nothing for himself, yet would help his friends achieve what he thought they needed. Those that appeared to be enjoying good fortune he would remind that they were buoyant about blessings that were only apparent, and which last for a short time. Those lamenting their poverty or complaining about exile or placing blame on old age or illness he would comfort with a laugh for not seeing how after a short time their troubles would cease and a kind of oblivion, of both the good and the bad, would soon fall upon them and with it a lasting freedom. To reconcile quarreling brothers and motion for peace between wives and their husbands was also of concern to him. He even on occasion talked down agitated crowds with fitting words and persuaded

ἐλευθερία μακρὰ πάντας ἐν ὀλίγῳ καταλήψεται. ἔμελεν δὲ αὐτῷ καὶ ἀδελφοὺς στασιάζοντας διαλλάττειν καὶ γυναιξὶ πρὸς τοὺς γεγαμηκότας εἰρήνην πρυτανεύειν· καί που καὶ δήμοις ταραττομένοις ἐμμελῶς διελέχθη καὶ τοὺς πλείστους αὐτῶν ἔπεισεν ὑπουργεῖν τῇ πατρίδι τὰ μέτρια.

Τοιοῦτός τις ἦν ὁ τρόπος τῆς φιλοσοφίας αὐτοῦ, πρᾶος καὶ ἥμερος καὶ φαιδρός· μόνον αὐτὸν ἠνία φίλου νόσος ἢ θάνατος, ὡς ἂν καὶ τὸ μέγιστον τῶν ἐν ἀνθρώποις ἀγαθῶν τὴν φιλίαν ἡγούμενον. καὶ διὰ τοῦτο φίλος μὲν ἦν ἅπασι καὶ οὐκ ἔστιν ὅντινα οὐκ οἰκεῖον ἐνόμιζεν, ἄνθρωπόν γε ὄντα, πλέον δὲ ἢ ἔλαττον ἔχαιρε συνὼν ἐνίοις αὐτῶν, μόνοις ἐξιστάμενος ὁπόσοι ἂν ἐδόκουν αὐτῷ ὑπὲρ τὴν τῆς θεραπείας ἐλπίδα διαμαρτάνειν. καὶ πάντα ταῦτα μετὰ Χαρίτων καὶ Ἀφροδίτης αὐτῆς ἔπραττέν τε καὶ ἔλεγεν, ὡς ἀεί, τὸ κωμικὸν ἐκεῖνο, τὴν πειθὼ τοῖς χείλεσιν αὐτοῦ ἐπικαθῆσθαι.

Τοιγαροῦν καὶ Ἀθηναίων ὅ τε σύμπας δῆμος καὶ οἱ ἐν τέλει ὑπερφυῶς ἐθαύμαζον αὐτὸν καὶ διετέλουν ὥς τινα τῶν κρειττόνων προσβλέποντες.

a good number of those people to serve their country measuredly.

That was what his brand of philosophy was like—meek, civilized, cheerful. The only thing that caused him grief was the sickness or death of a friend since he considered friendship the greatest human good. Accordingly, there was no one he did not include in his orbit, on the grounds that we are all human beings. He did, however, enjoy the company of some people more than others. He kept his distance only from those who seemed to him to have gone astray beyond hope of cure. Yet, in every instance he spoke and acted as if attended by the Graces and Aphrodite herself with the result that, to quote that quip from Old Comedy, "Persuasion took her seat upon his lips."[4]

Thus, the whole Athenian populace, including officials in government, admired him enormously and always regarded him as someone superior. At the beginning, however, he clashed with the majority and incurred a hatred owing to his frankness of speech and free way of living that was no less intense than what affected his predecessor Socrates. He had his own Anytus and Meletus who accused him of the same things the original ones did Socrates back then.[5] For they alleged he had never

καίτοι ἐν ἀρχῇ προσέκρουε τοῖς πολλοῖς αὐτῶν καὶ
μῖσος οὐ μεῖον τοῦ πρὸ αὐτοῦ παρὰ τοῖς πλήθεσιν
ἐκτήσατο ἐπί τε τῇ παρρησίᾳ καὶ ἐλευθερίᾳ, καί
τινες ἐπ' αὐτὸν συνέστησαν Ἄνυτοι καὶ Μέλητοι τὰ
αὐτὰ κατηγοροῦντες ἅπερ κἀκείνου οἱ τότε, ὅτι οὔτε
θύων ὤφθη πώποτε οὔτε ἐμυήθη μόνος ἁπάντων
ταῖς Ἐλευσινίαις· πρὸς ἅπερ ἀνδρείως μάλα στε-
φανωσάμενος καὶ καθαρὸν ἱμάτιον ἀναλαβὼν καὶ
παρελθὼν εἰς τὴν ἐκκλησίαν τὰ μὲν ἐμμελῶς, τὰ δὲ
καὶ τραχύτερον ἢ κατὰ τὴν ἑαυτοῦ προαίρεσιν ἀπε-
λογήσατο· πρὸς μὲν γὰρ τὸ μὴ τεθυκέναι πώποτε τῇ
Ἀθηνᾷ, Μὴ θαυμάσητε, ἔφη, ὦ ἄνδρες Ἀθηναῖοι, εἰ
μὴ πρότερον αὐτῇ ἔθυσα, οὐδὲν γὰρ δεῖσθαι αὐτὴν
τῶν παρ' ἐμοῦ θυσιῶν ὑπελάμβανον. πρὸς δὲ θάτε-
ρον, τὸ τῶν μυστηρίων, ταύτην ἔφη ἔχειν αἰτίαν τοῦ
μὴ κοινωνῆσαι σφίσι τῆς τελετῆς, ὅτι, ἄν τε φαῦλα
ᾖ τὰ μυστήρια, οὐ σιωπήσεται πρὸς τοὺς μηδέπω
μεμυημένους, ἀλλ' ἀποτρέψει αὐτοὺς τῶν ὀργίων,
ἄν τε καλά, πᾶσιν αὐτὰ ἐξαγορεύσει ὑπὸ φιλαν-
θρωπίας· ὥστε τοὺς Ἀθηναίους ἤδη λίθους ἐπ'
αὐτὸν ἐν ταῖν χεροῖν ἔχοντας πράους αὐτῷ καὶ ἵλεως
γενέσθαι αὐτίκα καὶ τὸ ἀπ' ἐκείνου ἀρξαμένους

been observed offering sacrifice and that he was the one person among them all not to have been initiated into the mysteries at Eleusis.[6] In response to these charges, Demonax bravely wreathed his head, donned a clean cloak, entered the Assembly and gave a defense speech, parts of which were well-tempered, while other bits were harsher than what was characteristic of his normal mode of life. To the charge of never having sacrificed to Athena he said, "Don't be so surprised, men of Athens, if I have not sacrificed to her previously, for I wasn't under the impression that she had need of offerings from me." To the other charge, about the mysteries, he gave this reason for not joining in the rites along with them, namely that if the mysteries were lousy, he would not keep that fact secret from those who had yet to be initiated but would direct them away from the rites. On the other hand, if they were good, he would tell everyone about them out of his love for humanity. Whereupon the Athenians, who already had stones in both hands ready to throw at him, immediately became gentle and kind toward him and from that time on began to honor, respect, and ultimately admire him—this in spite of the fact that the preamble he employed in his speech was rather trenchant: "Men of Athens," he said, "you see me

τιμᾶν καὶ αἰδεῖσθαι καὶ τὰ τελευταῖα θαυμάζειν, καίτοι εὐθὺς ἐν ἀρχῇ τῶν πρὸς αὐτοὺς λόγων τραχυτέρῳ ἐχρήσατο τῷ προοιμίῳ· Ἄνδρες γὰρ ἔφη Ἀθηναῖοι, ἐμὲ μὲν ὁρῶντες ἐστεφανωμένον ὑμεῖς ἤδη. κἀμὲ καταθύσατε, τὸ γὰρ πρότερον οὐκ ἐκαλλιερήσατε.

. . . . . .

Ἐβίου δὲ ἔτη ὀλίγου δέοντα τῶν ἑκατὸν ἄνοσος, ἄλυπος, οὐδένα ἐνοχλήσας τι ἢ αἰτήσας, φίλοις χρήσιμος, ἐχθρὸν οὐδένα οὐδεπώποτε ἐσχηκώς· καὶ τοσοῦτον ἔρωτα ἔσχον πρὸς αὐτὸν Ἀθηναῖοί τε αὐτοὶ καὶ ἅπασα ἡ Ἑλλάς, ὥστε παριόντι ὑπεξανίστασθαι μὲν τοὺς ἄρχοντας, σιωπὴν δὲ γίνεσθαι παρὰ πάντων. τὸ τελευταῖον δὲ ἤδη ὑπέργηρως ὢν ἄκλητος εἰς ἣν τύχοι παριὼν οἰκίαν ἐδείπνει καὶ ἐκάθευδε, τῶν ἐνοικούντων θεοῦ τινα ἐπιφάνειαν ἡγουμένων τὸ πρᾶγμα καί τινα ἀγαθὸν δαίμονα εἰσεληλυθέναι αὐτοῖς εἰς τὴν οἰκίαν. παριόντα δὲ αἱ ἀρτοπώλιδες ἀνθεῖλκον πρὸς αὑτὰς ἑκάστη ἀξιοῦσα παρ' αὑτῆς λαμβάνειν τῶν ἄρτων, καὶ τοῦτο εὐτυχίαν ἑαυτῆς ἡ δεδω-

now wreathed before you. Go ahead and sacrifice me, since your previous oblation clearly did not give you favorable omens!"[7]

[Lucian continues with a miscellany of Demonax's witty remarks, the "Attic charm" of which, to be frank, doesn't hold a candle to the quips of Diogenes included in selection nos. 1 and 7.]

He lived just shy of one hundred years without sickness or pain and without bothering or asking anything of anyone. He was all the while helpful to his friends and made an enemy of none. The Athenians and all of Greece felt such affection for him that the magistrates would fall silent and stand up in front of everyone when he passed by. Near the end, when he was extremely old, he would enter uninvited whatever house he happened upon to eat and sleep. The people whose house it was viewed the situation as virtually a divine epiphany and thought a good spirit had entered their home. When he passed by in the street, the women who sell bread would pull him over to themselves, each one thinking he should take some bread from her, and the one who had successfully given him her bread thought this was a stroke of good luck. Children, too, would bring him fruit and call him father. One time, when political strife took hold in Athens, he walked into

κυῖα ᾤετο. καὶ μὴν καὶ οἱ παῖδες ὀπώρας προσέφερον αὐτῷ πατέρα ὀνομάζοντες. στάσεως δέ ποτε Ἀθήνησι γενομένης εἰσῆλθεν εἰς τὴν ἐκκλησίαν καὶ φανεὶς μόνον σιωπᾶν ἐποίησεν αὐτούς· ὁ δὲ ἰδὼν ἤδη μετεγνωκότας οὐδὲν εἰπὼν καὶ αὐτὸς ἀπηλλάγη.

Ὅτε δὲ συνῆκεν οὐκέθ᾽ οἷός τε ὢν αὑτῷ ἐπικουρεῖν, εἰπὼν πρὸς τοὺς παρόντας τὸν ἐναγώνιον τῶν κηρύκων πόδα

Λήγει μὲν ἀγὼν τῶν καλλίστων
ἄθλων ταμίας, καιρὸς δὲ καλεῖ
μηκέτι μέλλειν,

καὶ πάντων ἀποσχόμενος ἀπῆλθεν τοῦ βίου φαιδρὸς καὶ οἷος ἀεὶ τοῖς ἐντυγχάνουσιν ἐφαίνετο. ὀλίγον δὲ πρὸ τῆς τελευτῆς ἐρομένου τινός, Περὶ ταφῆς τί κελεύεις; Μὴ πολυπραγμονεῖτε, ἔφη· ἡ γὰρ ὀδμή με θάψει. φαμένου δὲ ἐκείνου, Τί οὖν; οὐκ αἰσχρὸν ὀρνέοις καὶ κυσὶ βορὰν προτεθῆναι τηλικούτου ἀνδρὸς σῶμα; Καὶ μὴν οὐδὲν ἄτοπον, ἔφη, τοῦτο, εἰ μέλλω καὶ ἀποθανὼν ζῴοις τισὶ χρήσιμος ἔσεσθαι. οἱ μέντοι Ἀθηναῖοι καὶ ἔθαψαν αὐτὸν δημοσίᾳ μεγαλοπρεπῶς καὶ ἐπὶ πολὺ ἐπένθησαν, καὶ

the Assembly and just his appearance caused the parties to fall silent. When he saw that they had repented of their actions, he left, never having said a word himself.

When he realized he was no longer able to take care of himself he quoted to those who were present with him the verses recited by heralds at the Games:

> The contest to allocate
> the finest of prizes ends.
> When the moment for you sends,
> you should never hesitate.

And so, abstaining from all food, Demonax quit this life, looking cheerful and just like he always did to people who met him. When a short while before his death someone asked him, "What are your instructions for the funeral?" he replied, "Don't trouble yourselves. The stench will bury me!" "But isn't it disrespectful," the man countered, "for the body of a man like you to be laid out as food for birds and dogs?" "I see nothing strange in that," he replied, "if even in death I can be useful to the living." Nevertheless, the Athenians did bury him—magnificently and at public expense—and mourned him for quite some time. They genuflected at the

τὸν θᾶκον τὸν λίθινον, ἐφ᾽ οὗ εἰώθει ὁπότε κάμνοι ἀναπαύεσθαι, προσεκύνουν καὶ ἐστεφάνουν ἐς τιμὴν τοῦ ἀνδρός, ἡγούμενοι ἱερὸν εἶναι καὶ τὸν λίθον, ἐφ᾽ οὗ ἐκαθέζετο. ἐπὶ μὲν γὰρ τὴν ἐκφορὰν οὐκ ἔστιν ὅστις οὐκ ἀπήντησεν, καὶ μάλιστα τῶν φιλοσόφων· οὗτοι μέντοι ὑποδύντες ἐκόμιζον αὐτὸν ἄχρι πρὸς τὸν τάφον.

Ταῦτα ὀλίγα πάνυ ἐκ πολλῶν ἀπεμνημόνευσα, καὶ ἔστιν ἀπὸ τούτων τοῖς ἀναγινώσκουσι λογίζεσθαι ὁποῖος ἐκεῖνος ἀνὴρ ἐγένετο.

stone bench he used to rest on when he was tired
and festooned it with garlands in his honor, for they
thought that even the stone on which he used to sit
was sacred. There was no one who did not attend
his funeral. Philosophers were there in abundance.
Indeed, they were the ones who hoisted him upon
their shoulders and brought him out to the tomb.

These are but a few of many things I might have
mentioned. From them, though, readers will be
able to figure out for themselves what sort of man
he was.

6. A Passage to India

(Strabo, *Geography* 15.63–65)

In this passage the geographer Strabo (63 BCE–24 CE) presents an encounter between Onesicritus (360–290 BCE), a helmsman in Alexander the Great's fleet who happened also to be a follower of Diogenes, and a band of so-called "naked philosophers" (gymnosophists) from the Indian subcontinent. The inevitable mingling of peoples in the wake of Alexander's conquests provided fertile ground for the exchange and comparison of ideas. Another of Alexander's conscripts, Pyrrho of Elis (360–270 BCE), had a similar encounter with the gymnosophists (Diogenes Laertius 9.9)—in his case probably early practitioners of Buddhism—whose teachings influenced his formulation of Skepticism.[1]

The Indian sages get the better of Onesicritus here and show themselves to be more Cynic than the Cynics. Their practice of voluntary poverty and yogic austerity confirms the emperor Julian's surmise later (selection no. 9) that aspects of Cynicism are universal and of perennial concern. The sage Calanus's warning about environmental overreach, for example, is eerily prescient.

Ὀνησίκριτος δὲ πεμφθῆναί φησιν αὐτὸς διαλεξό-
μενος τοῖς σοφισταῖς τούτοις· ἀκούειν γὰρ τὸν
Ἀλέξανδρον, ὡς γυμνοὶ διατελοῖεν καὶ καρτερίας
ἐπιμελοῖντο οἱ ἄνθρωποι, ἐν τιμῇ τε ἄγοιντο πλεί-
στῃ, παρ' ἄλλους δὲ μὴ βαδίζοιεν κληθέντες, ἀλλὰ
κελεύοιεν ἐκείνους φοιτᾶν παρ' αὐτούς, εἴ του μετασχεῖν ἐθέλοιεν τῶν πραττομένων ἢ λεγομένων
ὑπ' αὐτῶν· τοιούτων δὴ ὄντων, ἐπειδὴ οὔτε αὐτῷ
πρέπειν ἐδόκει παρ' ἐκείνους φοιτᾶν οὔτε ἐκείνους βιάζεσθαι παρὰ τὰ πάτρια ποιεῖν τι ἄκοντας,
αὐτὸς ἔφη πεμφθῆναι·

καταλαβεῖν δὲ ἄνδρας πεντεκαίδεκα ἀπὸ στα-
δίων εἴκοσι τῆς πόλεως, ἄλλον ἐν ἄλλῳ σχήματι
ἑστῶτα ἢ καθήμενον ἢ κείμενον γυμνόν, ἀκίνητον
ἕως ἑσπέρας, εἶτ' ἀπερχόμενον εἰς τὴν πόλιν· χαλεπώτατον δ' εἶναι τὸ τὸν ἥλιον ὑπομεῖναι οὕτω
θερμόν, ὥστε τῶν ἄλλων μηδένα ὑπομένειν γυμνοῖς
ἐπιβῆναι τοῖς ποσὶ τῆς γῆς ῥᾳδίως κατὰ μεσημβρίαν.

Διαλεχθῆναι δ' ἑνὶ τούτων Καλάνῳ, ὃν καὶ συ-
νακολουθῆσαι τῷ βασιλεῖ μέχρι Περσίδος καὶ
ἀποθανεῖν τῷ πατρίῳ νόμῳ, τεθέντα ἐπὶ πυρκαϊάν·

Onesicritus relates that he was dispatched personally to interview these sophists, for Alexander had heard that there were people who went about their business naked, practiced self-mastery, and were held in the highest esteem. But they would not come to visit anyone by invitation. Rather they directed others to come visit *them* if they had interest in participating in their discussions and practices. Since those were the terms, and it struck Alexander as unseemly for him to go visit or to force them to violate their ancestral customs against their will, Onesicritus was sent.

About a quarter mile from the city, Onesicritus says he came upon fifteen men, each standing in his own respective posture, or sitting, or lying down naked, motionless, till evening, at which time they would return to town. The sun was so hot, he says, and so exceedingly hard to endure that at midday nobody else could bear to walk on the ground barefoot with ease.

Onesicritus struck up a conversation with one of the sages, Calanus, who later accompanied Alexander as far as Persia and died there according to the ancestral custom by being placed upon a pyre.[2] Calanus happened to be lying on stones at that moment, so Onesicritus approached and greeted him,

τότε δ' ἐπὶ λίθων τυχεῖν κείμενον· προσιὼν οὖν καὶ
προσαγορεύσας εἰπεῖν ἔφη, διότι πεμφθείη παρὰ
τοῦ βασιλέως ἀκροασόμενος τῆς σοφίας αὐτῶν, καὶ
ἀπαγγελῶν πρὸς αὐτόν· εἰ οὖν μηδεὶς εἴη φθόνος,
ἕτοιμος εἴη μετασχεῖν τῆς ἀκροάσεως· ἰδόντα δ'
ἐκεῖνον χλαμύδα καὶ καυσίαν φοροῦντα καὶ κρη-
πῖδα, καταγελάσαντα, Τὸ παλαιόν, φάναι, πάντ'
ἦν ἀλφίτων καὶ ἀλεύρων πλήρη, καθάπερ νῦν κό-
νεως· καὶ κρῆναι δ' ἔρρεον, αἱ μὲν ὕδατος, γάλακτος δ' ἄλλαι, καὶ ὁμοίως μέλιτος, αἱ δ' οἴνου, τινὲς
δ' ἐλαίου· ὑπὸ πλησμονῆς δ' οἱ ἄνθρωποι καὶ τρυφῆς εἰς ὕβριν ἐξέπεσον. Ζεὺς δὲ μισήσας τὴν κα-
τάστασιν ἠφάνισε πάντα καὶ διὰ πόνου τὸν βίον
ἀπέδειξε. σωφροσύνης δὲ καὶ τῆς ἄλλης ἀρετῆς
παρελθούσης εἰς μέσον, πάλιν εὐπορία τῶν ἀγαθῶν
ὑπῆρξεν. ἐγγὺς δ' ἐστὶν ἤδη νυνὶ κόρου καὶ ὕβρεως
τὸ πρᾶγμα, κινδυνεύει τε ἀφανισμὸς τῶν ὄντων
γενέσθαι. ταῦτα εἰπόντα κελεύειν, εἰ βούλοιτο
ἀκροάσασθαι, καταθέμενον τὴν σκευὴν γυμνὸν ἐπὶ
τῶν αὐτῶν λίθων κείμενον, μετέχειν τῶν λόγων.

saying he had been sent by Alexander to inquire about their wisdom and to report back, and, if there were no objections, he was ready to hear what he had to say. Calanus, however, took one look at the cloak, broad hat, and high boots that Onesicritus was wearing and laughed in his face, saying, "In ancient times, everything teemed with barley and wheat. These days all is dust. Springs used to gush with water and milk—honey, too—and with wine and olive oil. But greed and luxury caused people to become arrogant. Disgusted by this state of affairs, Zeus[3] annihilated all of it, and subjected people to a life of toil. When self-restraint and the other virtues came front and center again, however, ready access to good things reemerged. And yet, excess and arrogance are once again close at hand and there is a risk that everything will be wiped out."[4] When Calanus had finished speaking, he urged Onesicritus, if he wanted to hear more, to take off his clothes and lie down naked on the same stones as he to engage in discussion.

Onesicritus was at a loss for what to do, but Mandanis, who was the eldest and wisest in the group, rebuffed Calanus for his own arrogance, which seemed especially arrogant seeing that he had just condemned arrogance. He called Onesicritus

ἀπορουμένου δὲ αὐτοῦ, Μάνδανιν, ὅσπερ ἦν
πρεσβύτατος καὶ σοφώτατος αὐτῶν, τὸν μὲν ἐπι-
πλῆξαι ὡς ὑβριστήν, καὶ ταῦτα ὕβρεως κατηγορή-
σαντα, αὐτὸν δὲ προσκαλέσασθαι καὶ εἰπεῖν, ὡς
τὸν μὲν βασιλέα ἐπαινοίη, διότι ἀρχὴν τοσαύτην
διοικῶν ἐπιθυμοίη σοφίας· μόνον γὰρ ἴδοι αὐτὸν
ἐν ὅπλοις φιλοσοφοῦντα· ὠφελιμώτατον δ᾽ εἴη
τῶν ἁπάντων, εἰ οἱ τοιοῦτοι φρονοῖεν, οἷς πάρεστι
δύναμις τοὺς μὲν ἑκουσίους πείθειν σωφρονεῖν,
τοὺς δ᾽ ἀκουσίους ἀναγκάζειν· αὐτῷ δὲ συγγνώμη
εἴη, εἰ δι᾽ ἑρμηνέων τριῶν διαλεγόμενος, πλὴν
φωνῆς μηδὲν συνιέντων πλέον ἢ οἱ πολλοί, μηδὲν
ἰσχύσει τῆς ὠφελείας ἐπίδειξιν ποιήσασθαι· ὅμοιον
γάρ, ὡς ἂν εἰ διὰ βορβόρου καθαρὸν ἀξιοῖ τις ὕδωρ
ῥεῖν.

over to him and praised Alexander in so far as, although he was administering so great an empire, he was still eager for wisdom, the only philosopher-in-arms, Mandanis said, he had ever seen, adding that it would be the most useful thing in the world if people of such a mindset and who held power would persuade the willing—and compel the unwilling—to a life of moderation; and he asked for forgiveness if he proved unable to reveal anything useful himself, seeing that he was communicating through three interpreters, who, apart from knowing the language, had not a whit more knowledge than the average person. That, he said, was like someone expecting water to flow clean through mud.

The gist of what Mandanis said, however, was that the best doctrine is one that aims to free the soul from pleasure and pain, and that pain and hardship are different things. One is inimical to us, the other our friend. They train their bodies, he said, with a view to enduring physical hardship so that their intellects might be strengthened. They are better able thereby to settle disagreements and become good advisers to all in matters both public and private. Indeed, he said he had just now advised Taxiles[5] to welcome Alexander on the grounds that

Τὰ γοῦν λεχθέντα εἰς τοῦτ᾽ ἔφη συντείνειν, ὡς εἴη λόγος ἄριστος, ὃς ἡδονὴν καὶ λύπην ψυχῆς ἀφαιρήσεται· καὶ ὅτι λύπη καὶ πόνος διαφέρει· τὸ μὲν γὰρ πολέμιον, τὸ δὲ φίλιον αὐτοῖς, τά γε σώματα ἀσκοῦσι πρὸς πόνον, ἵν᾽ αἱ γνῶμαι ῥωννύοιντο, ἀφ᾽ ὧν καὶ στάσεις παύοιεν καὶ σύμβουλοι πᾶσιν ἀγαθῶν παρεῖεν καὶ κοινῇ καὶ ἰδίᾳ· καὶ δὴ καὶ Ταξίλῃ νῦν συμβουλεύσειε δέχεσθαι τὸν Ἀλέξανδρον· κρείττω μὲν γὰρ αὐτοῦ δεξάμενον εὖ πείσεσθαι, χείρω δὲ εὖ διαθήσειν.

ταῦτ᾽ εἰπόντα ἐξερέσθαι, εἰ καὶ ἐν τοῖς Ἕλλησι λόγοι τοιοῦτοι λέγοιντο· εἰπόντος δ᾽, ὅτι καὶ Πυθαγόρας τοιαῦτα λέγοι, κελεύοι τε ἐμψύχων ἀπέχεσθαι, καὶ Σωκράτης καὶ Διογένης, οὗ καὶ αὐτὸς ἀκροάσαιτο, ἀποκρίνασθαι, ὅτι τἆλλα μὲν νομίζοι φρονίμως αὐτοῖς δοκεῖν, ἓν δ᾽ ἁμαρτάνειν, νόμον πρὸ τῆς φύσεως τιθεμένους· οὐ γὰρ ἂν αἰσχύνεσθαι γυμνούς, ὥσπερ αὐτόν, διάγειν, ἀπὸ λιτῶν ζῶντας· καὶ γὰρ οἰκίαν ἀρίστην εἶναι, ἥτις ἂν ἐπισκευῆς ἐλαχίστης δέηται·

ἔφη δ᾽ αὐτοὺς καὶ τῶν περὶ φύσιν πολλὰ ἐξετάσαι καὶ προσημασιῶν, ὄμβρων, αὐχμῶν, νόσων· ἀπιόντας δ᾽ εἰς τὴν πόλιν κατὰ τὰς ἀγορὰς σκεδάννυσθαι· ὅτῳ δ᾽ ἂν κομίζοντι σῦκα ἢ βότρυς παρατύχωσι, λαμβάνειν δωρεὰν παρέχοντος· εἰ δ᾽ ἔλαιον εἴη, καταχεῖσθαι αὐτῶν καὶ ἀλείφεσθαι· ἅπασαν δὲ πλουσίαν οἰκίαν ἀνεῖσθαι αὐτοῖς μέχρι γυναι-

if he were receiving a man better than himself, he would be well treated, but if worse, he might improve him.

Mandanis then asked Onesicritus if any such doctrines were held among the Greeks, and Onesicritus replied that Pythagoras taught similar things, and that he insisted on abstention from animal products; Socrates taught similar things, too, and Diogenes, whose disciple he, Onesicritus, had been. Mandanis answered that the Greeks seemed to him sensible overall, but wrong to defer to Custom over Nature. Why else, he said, were they ashamed to live, as he did, unclothed and on simple fare? After all, even in the case of shelter, he said, the best house is the one requiring the least maintenance.

Onesicritus says the gymnosophists also investigate natural phenomena like signs, rains, droughts, and diseases. When they return to the city, they scatter themselves across the marketplaces, and if they should meet someone carrying grapes or figs, they receive some from him as an offering; if it's oil, it is poured over them and they are anointed with it. Wealthy households provide them full access, too, even to the women's apartments; they enter and share in meals and discussion. They

κωνίτιδος, εἰσιόντας δὲ δείπνου κοινωνεῖν καὶ
λόγων· αἴσχιστον δ᾽ αὐτοῖς νομίζεσθαι νόσον σω-
ματικήν· τὸν δ᾽ ὑπονοήσαντα καθ᾽ αὑτοῦ τοῦτο,
ἐξάγειν ἑαυτὸν διὰ πυρός, νήσαντα πυράν, ὑπα-
λειψάμενον δὲ καὶ καθίσαντα ἐπὶ τὴν πυρὰν ὑφά-
ψαι κελεύειν, ἀκίνητον δὲ καίεσθαι.

consider bodily sickness most disgraceful. If someone suspects he's ill, he commits suicide by fire. He piles up a funeral bier, anoints himself with oil, then, taking his seat upon it, orders the pyre to be kindled and burns up without flinching.

7. Best in Show

(Dio Chrysostom, Oration 9, "Isthmian Discourse")

Cynicism frequently analogizes its practices to athletic endeavor. Its keyword and core concept— askēsis *("training"), whence the word "ascetic"—is in fact drawn from the world of Greek sport. In this passage, Dio of Prusa (40–115 CE), himself an itinerant Cynic and nicknamed "golden-tongued" (Chrysostom) for his eloquence, takes this ball, as it were, and runs with it. The "display speech" translated here describes Diogenes's visit to the athletic contests and public festival at Isthmia, near Corinth, and what he did and said among the crowds there. Diogenes, the bemused spectator, is presented as the true athlete in the competition for virtuous living. The praise heaped on animals at the expense of human beings in this piece is also characteristic of Cynic sensibilities and indirectly foreshadows the contemporary interest in the intelligence and agency of nonhuman actors in an increasingly post-human world.*

Ἰσθμίων ὄντων κατέβη Διογένης εἰς τὸν Ἰσθμόν, ὡς
ἔοικεν, ἐν Κορίνθῳ διατρίβων. παρετύγχανε δὲ ταῖς
πανηγύρεσιν οὐχ ὧνπερ οἱ πολλοὶ ἕνεκα, βουλόμενοι θεάσασθαι τοὺς ἀθλητὰς καὶ ἵνα ἐμπλησθῶσιν,
ἀλλ' ἐπισκοπῶν οἶμαι τοὺς ἀνθρώπους καὶ τὴν
ἄνοιαν αὐτῶν ᾔδει γὰρ ὅτι φανερώτατοί εἰσιν ἐν
ταῖς ἑορταῖς καὶ ταῖς πανηγύρεσιν· ἐν δὲ πολέμῳ
καὶ στρατοπέδῳ λανθάνουσι μᾶλλον διὰ τὸ κινδυ-
νεύειν καὶ φοβεῖσθαι. . . .

διὰ ταῦτα παρέβαλλεν εἰς τὰς πανηγύρεις. ἔλεγε
δὲ ἐπισκώπτων, ὅτε ἐπιπλήττοιτο τὸ τοῦ κυνός·
τοὺς γὰρ κύνας ἕπεσθαι μὲν εἰς τὰς πανηγύρεις,
μηδένα δὲ ἀδικεῖν τῶν ἐκεῖ γιγνομένων, ὑλακτεῖν
δὲ καὶ μάχεσθαι τοῖς κακούργοις καὶ λῃσταῖς, καὶ
ὅταν οἱ ἄνθρωποι μεθυσθέντες καθεύδωσιν, αὐτοὺς
ἐγρηγορότας φυλάττειν.

Ὡς δὲ ἐφάνη ἐν τῇ πανηγύρει, Κορινθίων μὲν
οὐδεὶς αὐτῷ προσεῖχε τὸν νοῦν, ὅτι πολλάκις αὐτὸν
ἑώρων ἐν τῇ πόλει καὶ περὶ τὸ Κράνειον. . . . Τῶν δὲ
ἄλλων οἱ μακρόθεν μάλιστα προσῄεσαν πρὸς αὐτόν,
ἀπὸ τῆς Ἰωνίας τε καὶ Σικελίας καὶ Ἰταλίας ὅσοι

The Isthmian Games were on,[1] so Diogenes, who was living in Corinth at the time, so it seems, went down to the Isthmus. But he did not attend the festivals for the same reasons as most people do. The masses want to watch the athletes and to eat and drink their fill. Diogenes, I reckon, went as an observer of people and their folly. For he knew that people are most forthcoming at feasts and festivals, whereas in battle or in camp, they're cagier on account of the danger and fear involved. . . .

It was for this reason, then, that he would make the rounds at festivals. Whenever he was reproved for behaving like a dog, he used to say jokingly in self-defense that dogs, too, follow the festival circuit, but none of them does any harm to those in attendance. Rather, they bark at or fight off wrongdoers and thieves. And whenever the humans get drunk and fall asleep, they stay awake and stand guard.

Anyhow, when he showed up at the Isthmian Games, no one from Corinth paid him any heed, for they often saw him in the city and in the Craneum there. . . . People from afar, however, flocked to him—citizens in attendance from Ionia and Sicily and Italy, even some from Libya, Massalia,[2] and Borysthenes.[3] All of these people, though, were more interested in setting eyes on him or hearing him

παρῆσαν καὶ τῶν ἐκ Λιβύης τινὲς καὶ τῶν ἐκ Μασ-
σαλίας καὶ ἀπὸ Βορυσθένους, οὗτοι δὴ πάντες ἰδεῖν
βουλόμενοι μᾶλλον αὐτὸν καὶ βραχύ τι ἀκοῦσαι λέ-
γοντος, ὡς ἔχοιεν ἀπαγγέλλειν ἑτέροις ἢ βελτίους
γενέσθαι. ἐδόκει γὰρ ἱκανὸς εἶναι λοιδορῆσαι καὶ
τοῖς ἐρωτῶσιν ἀποκρίνασθαι πρὸς ἔπος. ὥσπερ οὖν
τοῦ Ποντικοῦ μέλιτος γεύεσθαι ἐπιχειροῦσιν οἱ
ἄπειροι, γευσάμενοι δὲ παραχρῆμα ἐξέπτυσαν δυσ-
σχεράναντες, ὅτι πικρόν ἐστι καὶ ἀηδές, οὕτως
καὶ τοῦ Διογένους ἀποπειρᾶσθαι μὲν ἤθελον διὰ
πολυπραγμοσύνην, ἐλεγχόμενοι δὲ ἀπεστρέφοντο
καὶ ἔφευγον. καὶ ἄλλων μὲν ἥδοντο λοιδορουμένων,
αὐτοὶ δὲ ἐφοβοῦντο καὶ ἀνεχώρουν. καὶ εἰ μὲν
ἔσκωπτέ τε καὶ ἔπαιζεν, ὥσπερ εἰώθει ἐνίοτε,
ὑπερφυῶς ἔχαιρον, ἀνατειναμένου δὲ καὶ σπου-
δάσαντος οὐχ ὑπέμενον τὴν παρρησίαν· καθάπερ
οἶμαι τὰ παιδία προσπαίζοντα ἥδεται τοῖς γενναίοις
κυσίν, ἐπειδὰν δὲ χαλεπήνῃ καὶ ὑλάξῃ μεῖζον, ἐξεπλάγη καὶ τῷ δέει τέθνηκε.

speak so that they could tell others about it than in becoming better persons themselves. For he had a reputation for being good at casting aspersions or answering back his interrogators on the spot. Just as those unfamiliar with Pontic honey, upon getting a taste of it, spit it out in disgust because it is bitter, not sweet,[4] people were eager to test Diogenes out of curiosity, but then, when cross-examined by him, they would turn tail and run. When others were being reviled, of course, it was fun, but for their own sakes they were afraid and kept their distance. If he told jokes and played the jester, as he sometimes did, people loved it to no end. But when he got worked up and serious, they couldn't abide his frank manner of speaking. It's the same, I think, with children: they enjoy playing with well-behaved dogs, but when a dog gets rough or barks a bit loud, they're shaken and scared to death.

At the Isthmian Games, too, Diogenes displayed the same behavior as always, giving no thought to changing his ways, regardless of whether someone among those present praised or blamed him, not even if it were someone rich or reputable, or if a military commander or potentate approached to speak with him, or if it were someone dirt poor and ordinary. When the poor and ordinary said stupid

Καὶ τότε ἐκεῖνος ἐποίει ταῦτά, οὐδὲν μεταστρε-
φόμενος οὐδὲ φροντίζων εἴτε ἐπαινοίη τις αὐτὸν
εἴτε καὶ ψέγοι τῶν παρόντων, οὐδὲ εἰ τῶν πλου-
σίων τε καὶ ἐνδόξων ἢ στρατηγὸς ἢ δυνάστης δι-
αλέγοιτο προσελθὼν ἢ τῶν πάνυ φαύλων τε καὶ
πενήτων· ἀλλὰ τῶν μὲν τοιούτων ληρούντων ἐνίοτε
κατεφρόνει, τοὺς δὲ σεμνοὺς εἶναι βουλομένους καὶ
μέγα φρονοῦντας ἐφ᾽ αὑτοῖς διὰ πλοῦτον ἢ γένος ἢ
ἄλλην τινὰ δύναμιν, τούτους μάλιστα ἐπίεζε καὶ
ἐκόλαζε πάντα τρόπον. τινὲς μὲν οὖν αὐτὸν ἐθαύμαζον ὡς σοφώτατον πάντων, τισὶ δὲ μαίνεσθαι ἐδόκει,
πολλοὶ δὲ κατεφρόνουν ὡς πτωχοῦ τε καὶ οὐδενὸς
ἀξίου, τινὲς δ᾽ ἐλοιδόρουν, οἱ δὲ προπηλακίζειν
ἐπεχείρουν, ὀστᾶ ῥιπτοῦντες πρὸ τῶν ποδῶν ὥσπερ
τοῖς κυσίν, οἱ δὲ καὶ τοῦ τρίβωνος ἥπτοντο προσιό-
ντες, πολλοὶ δὲ οὐκ εἴων ἀλλ᾽ ἠγανάκτουν, καθάπερ Ὅμηρός φησι τὸν Ὀδυσσέα προσπαίζειν τοὺς
μνηστῆρας· κἀκεῖνον πρὸς ὀλίγας ἡμέρας ἐνεγκεῖν
τὴν ἀκολασίαν αὐτῶν καὶ τὴν ὕβριν, ὁ δὲ ὅμοιος ἦν
ἐν ἅπαντι· τῷ ὄντι γὰρ ἐῴκει βασιλεῖ καὶ δεσπότῃ,
πτωχοῦ στολὴν ἔχοντι, κἄπειτα ἐν ἀνδραπόδοις
τε καὶ δούλοις αὑτοῦ στρεφομένῳ τρυφῶσι καὶ
ἀγνοοῦσιν ὅστις ἐστί, καὶ ῥᾳδίως φέροντι μεθύο-
ντας ἀνθρώπους καὶ μαινομένους ὑπὸ ἀγνοίας καὶ
ἀμαθίας.

things, he was sometimes disdainful toward them. But those wishing to be respected or who thought a lot of themselves because of their wealth, birth, or some other distinction, these he pressed hard and punished in any way he could. Some admired him therefore as the wisest man in the world. Others, however, thought him mad. Many despised him as a worthless beggar and mocked him. Yet others tried to humiliate him by throwing bones at his feet as you would to a dog. Still others drew near to lay hands on his cloak. Many didn't give him the time of day but did find him annoying— all exactly how Homer describes the Suitors taunting Odysseus.[5] He, too, endured their excess and insolence for a few days. Diogenes was similar in every respect. For indeed Diogenes was like a king and master dressed in a beggar's cloak, who, twisting and turning his way among his own servants and slaves—they luxuriating, unaware of who he was—bore their drunkenness and madness easily, their behavior sprung from ignorance and stupidity.

For the most part, the judges of the Isthmian Games and whoever else was esteemed and powerful were at a total loss about what to do. They withdrew to themselves whenever Diogenes was

Ὅλως δὲ οἵ τε ἀθλοθέται τῶν Ἰσθμίων καὶ τῶν ἄλλων ὅσοι ἔντιμοι καὶ δυνατοὶ σφόδρα ἠποροῦντο καὶ συνεστέλλοντο κατ᾽ ἐκεῖνον ὁπότε γένοιντο, καὶ πάντες οὗτοι σιγῇ παρῄεσαν ὑποβλέποντες αὐτόν. ἐπεὶ δὲ καὶ ἐστεφανώσατο τῆς πίτυος, πέμψαντες οἱ Κορίνθιοι τῶν ὑπηρετῶν τινας ἐκέλευον ἀποθέσθαι τὸν στέφανον καὶ μηδὲν παράνομον ποιεῖν. ὁ δὲ ἤρετο αὐτοὺς διὰ τί παράνομόν ἐστιν αὐτὸν ἐστεφανῶσθαι τῆς πίτυος, ἄλλους δὲ οὐ παράνομον. εἶπεν οὖν τις αὐτῶν, Ὅτι οὐ νενίκηκας, ὦ Διόγενες. ὁ δέ, Πολλούς γε, εἶπεν, ἀνταγωνιστὰς καὶ μεγάλους, οὐχ οἷα ταῦτά ἐστι τὰ ἀνδράποδα τὰ νῦν ἐνταῦθα παλαίοντα καὶ δισκεύοντα καὶ τρέχοντα, τῷ παντὶ δὲ χαλεπωτέρους, πενίαν καὶ φυγὴν καὶ ἀδοξίαν, ἔτι δὲ ὀργήν τε καὶ λύπην καὶ ἐπιθυμίαν καὶ φόβον καὶ τὸ πάντων ἀμαχώτατον θηρίον, ὕπουλον καὶ μαλθακόν, ἡδονήν· ἧ οὐδεὶς οὔτε τῶν Ἑλλήνων οὔτε τῶν βαρβάρων ἀξιοῖ μάχεαθαι καὶ περιεῖναι τῇ ψυχῇ κρατήσας, ἀλλὰ πάντες ἥττηνται καὶ ἀπειρήκασι πρὸς τὸν ἀγῶνα τοῦτον, Πέρσαι καὶ Μῆδοι καὶ Σύροι καὶ Μακεδόνες καὶ Ἀθηναῖοι καὶ Λακεδαιμόνιοι, πλὴν ἐμοῦ. πότερον οὖν

around or walked by in silence, giving him menacing looks. But when Diogenes went so far as to place the victory crown of pine boughs on his own head, the Corinthian delegation sent some of its support staff to insist he take it off and do nothing unlawful. He, however, asked them why it was unlawful for him to wear the pine-bough crown but not unlawful for others. In response one of them said, "Because, Diogenes, you have not won a victory." "In fact," he said in reply, "I have defeated many great competitors, not like these slaves wrestling here now, tossing the discus and running races, but adversaries far more formidable in every way—poverty and exile and disrepute; and more formidable still—anger and pain and desire and fear; and, the most difficult monster of all to handle—soft to the touch and festering inside—*pleasure*—which no Greek or barbarian can claim to have bested by strength of soul. Rather, all have been worsted and succumbed in *that* contest—Persians, Medes, Syrians, Macedonians, Athenians, Spartans—all, except me. Do I not then seem to you as worthy of the pine-bough crown, or will you take it away and give it to the man packed with the most meat? Report back to those who sent you and tell them these things and also this: that *they*

ὑμῖν ἄξιος δοκῶ τῆς πίτυος, ἢ λαβόντες αὐτὴν δώ-
σετε τῷ πλείστων κρεῶν γέμοντι; ταῦτα οὖν
ἀπαγγέλλετε τοῖς πέμψασι καὶ ὅτι αὐτοὶ παρανο-
μοῦσιν· οὐ γὰρ νικήσαντες οὐδένα ἀγῶνα περιέρ-
χονται στεφάνους ἔχοντες· καὶ ὅτι ἐνδοξότερα
πεποίηκα τὰ Ἴσθμια κατακρατήσας αὐτὸς τὸν
στέφανον, καὶ ὅτι οὐ τοῖς ἀνθρώποις, ἀλλὰ ταῖς
αἰξὶ δηλαδὴ περιμάχητον αὐτὸν εἶναι δεῖ.

Μετὰ δὲ τοῦτο ἰδών τινα ἐκ τοῦ σταδίου βαδίζοντα μετὰ πολλοῦ πλήθους καὶ μηδὲ ἐπιβαίνοντα τῆς
γῆς, ἀλλὰ ὑψηλὸν φερόμενον ὑπὸ τοῦ ὄχλου, τοὺς
δέ τινας ἐπακολουθοῦντας καὶ βοῶντας, ἄλλους δὲ
πηδῶντας ὑπὸ χαρᾶς καὶ τὰς χεῖρας αἴροντας πρὸς
τὸν οὐρανόν, τοὺς δὲ ἐπιβάλλοντας αὐτῷ στεφάνους καὶ ταινίας, ὅτε ἐδυνήθη προσελθεῖν, ἤρετο τίς
ἐστιν ὁ θόρυβος ὁ περὶ αὐτὸν καὶ τί συνέβη. ὁ δὲ
ἔφη, Νικῶμεν, Διόγενες, τῶν ἀνδρῶν τὸ στάδιον.
Τοῦτο δὲ τί ἐστιν; εἶπεν· οὐ γὰρ δὴ φρονιμώτερος
γέγονας οὐδὲ μικρόν, ὅτι ἔφθασας τοὺς συντρέχο-
ντας, οὐδὲ σωφρονέστερος νῦν ἢ πρότερον οὐδὲ
δειλὸς ἧττον, οὐδ᾽ ἔλαττον ἀλγεῖς οὐδ᾽ ἐλαττόνων

are the ones who are breaking the law. For they waltz about wearing crowns yet are victorious in no real contest. And tell them, too, that I have made the Isthmian Games more reputable by having awarded myself the crown; and that, obviously, a crown of pine boughs is for goats to fight over, not people."

After this encounter, he saw a man striding from the running track attended by a large crowd. In fact, the man was not even treading the ground, but was being borne high aloft by the throng. Some people were following along and cheering. Others were jumping for joy and lifting their hands to heaven. Still others were tossing garland crowns and ribbons on his head. When Diogenes was able to approach, he asked what the ruckus for this guy was all about and what had happened. "We have won!" the man said, "The men's two-hundred-yard dash!" "And what kind of achievement is that?" Diogenes replied. "For you have not become even a tad more intelligent for having beat your fellow runners, nor more moderate now than before, nor less cowardly or less dissatisfied. And you will not need fewer things in the future and will not live freer from pain." "Maybe so," he replied, "but I am the fastest man among all the other Greeks." "But

δεήσῃ τὸ λοιπὸν οὐδὲ ἀλυπότερον βιώσῃ. Μὰ Δία, εἶπεν, ἀλλὰ τῶν ἄλλων Ἑλλήνων ταχύτατός εἰμι πάντων. Ἀλλ' οὐ τῶν λαγῶν, ἔφη ὁ Διογένης, οὐδὲ τῶν ἐλάφων· καίτοι ταῦτα τὰ θηρία, πάντων τάχιστά, ἐστι καὶ δειλότατα, καὶ τοὺς ἀνθρώπους καὶ τοὺς κύνας καὶ τοὺς ἀετοὺς φοβεῖται, καὶ ζῇ βίον ἄθλιον. οὐκ οἶσθα, ἔφη, ὅτι τὸ τάχος δειλίας σημεῖόν ἐστι; τοῖς γὰρ αὐτοῖς ζῴοις συμβέβηκε ταχίστοις τε εἶναι καὶ ἀνανδροτάτοις. ὁ γοῦν Ἡρακλῆς διὰ τὸ βραδύτερος εἶναι πολλῶν καὶ μὴ δύνασθαι κατὰ πόδας αἱρεῖν τοὺς κακούργους, διὰ τοῦτο ἐφόρει τόξα καὶ τούτοις ἐχρῆτο ἐπὶ τοὺς φεύγοντας. καὶ ὅς, Ἀλλὰ τὸν Ἀχιλλέα, ἔφη, ταχὺν ὄντα φησὶν ὁ ποιητὴς ἀνδρειότατον εἶναι. Καὶ πῶς, ἔφη, οἶσθα ὅτι ταχὺς ἦν ὁ Ἀχιλλεύς; τὸν μὲν γὰρ Ἕκτορα ἑλεῖν οὐκ ἐδύνατο κατὰ τὴν ἡμέραν ὅλην διώκων.

Οὐκ αἰσχύνῃ, ἔφη, ἐπὶ πράγματι σεμνυνόμενος ἐν ᾧ τῶν φαυλοτάτων θηρίων χείρων πέφυκας; οἶμαι γάρ σε μηδὲ ἀλώπεκα δύνασθαι φθάσαι. πόσον δέ τι καὶ ἔφθασας; Παρ' ὀλίγον, εἶπεν, ὦ Διόγενες. τοῦτο γάρ τοι καὶ τὸ θαυμαστὸν ἐγένετο τῆς νίκης. Ὥστε, ἔφη, παρ' ἓν βῆμα εὐδαίμων γέγονας. Ἅπαντες γὰρ οἱ κράτιστοι ἦμεν οἱ τρέχοντες. Οἱ δὲ κόρυδοι πόσῳ τινὶ θᾶττον ὑμῶν διέρχονται τὸ στάδιον; Πτηνοὶ γάρ εἰσιν, εἶπεν. Οὐκοῦν, ἔφη ὁ Διογένης, εἴπερ τὸ ταχύτατον εἶναι κράτι-

not faster than rabbits," Diogenes retorted, "nor than deer. And yet these creatures, the fastest of all, are also the flightiest. They are afraid of people, dogs, and eagles, and live miserably. Do you not see," he added, "that speed is an index of cowardice? For it is the nature of things among animals that the fastest are also the most slavish. Heracles, on the same principle, because he was slower than many and unable to catch bad guys on foot used to carry a bow and plied that against those who ran from him." To this the other man replied, "But the poet says Achilles was fast, and the bravest."[6] "How do you know Achilles was fast?" Diogenes replied. "He was unable to catch Hector, and he pursued him for an entire day!"[7]

"Are you not ashamed," Diogenes continued, "to puff yourself up over an activity at which you are naturally worse than the lowliest animals? I doubt you could even beat a fox. And how much did you win by anyhow?" "Just a little, Diogenes," he said. "That's what made my victory so amazing, of course." "So," Diogenes replied, "you are fortunate by one stride." "Yes, but we were all the best runners." "But how much more quickly does a lark get across the length of the course than you?" "Well, larks have wings," he said. "But if the swift-

στόν ἐστι, πολὺ βέλτιον κόρυδον εἶναι σχεδὸν ἢ ἄν-
θρωπον· ὥστε τὰς ἀηδόνας οὐδέν τι δεῖ οἰκτίρειν
οὐδὲ τοὺς ἔποπας, ὅτι ὄρνιθες ἐγένοντο ἐξ ἀνθρώπων, ὡς ὑπὸ τοῦ μύθου λέλεκται. Ἀλλ᾽ ἐγώ, ἔφη,
ἄνθρωπος ὢν ἀνθρώπων ταχύτατός εἰμι. Τί δέ;
οὐχὶ καὶ ἐν τοῖς μύρμηξιν, εἶπεν, εἰκὸς ἄλλον ἄλλου
ταχύτερον εἶναι; μὴ οὖν θαυμάζουσιν αὐτόν; ἢ οὐ
δοκεῖ σοι γελοῖον εἶναι εἴ τις ἐθαύμαζε μύρμηκα ἐπὶ
τάχει; τί δέ; εἰ χωλοὶ πάντες ἦσαν οἱ τρέχοντες,
ἐχρῆν σε μέγα φρονεῖν ὅτι χωλοὺς χωλὸς ἔφθης;

Τοιαῦτα δὲ πρὸς τὸν ἄνθρωπον διαλεγόμενος
πολλοὺς ἐποίησε τῶν παρόντων καταφρονῆσαι τοῦ
πράγματος κἀκεῖνον αὐτὸν λυπούμενον ἀπελθεῖν
καὶ πολὺ ταπεινότερον. τοῦτο δὲ οὐ μικρὸν παρεῖχε
τοῖς ἀνθρώποις, ὁπότε ἴδοι τινὰ μάτην ἐπαιρόμενον
καὶ διὰ πρᾶγμα οὐδενὸς ἄξιον ἔξω τοῦ φρονεῖν,
συστείλας ἐπὶ βραχὺ καὶ ἀφελὼν μικρόν τι τῆς
ἀνοίας, ὥσπερ οἱ τὰ πεφυσημένα καὶ οἰδοῦντα νύ-
ξαντες ἢ στίξαντες.

est thing is superior," Diogenes retorted, "it is therefore probably much better to be a lark than to be a human. Consequently, there's no need to pity the nightingale or hoopoe because they were transformed from humans into birds as recounted in the myth."[8] "But I," the other replied, "am a human being, and in my capacity as a human being, am the fastest." "But what of it?" Diogenes replied. "In the ant kingdom, too, is it not likely that one ant is faster than another? And yet, surely, they don't admire the speedy one. Does it not seem laughable to you to admire an ant for speed? What is more, if all the runners had been cripples, would it have been right for you to boast, because you, in your capacity as a cripple yourself, had beaten cripples?"

By conversing with the man in this way Diogenes made many in attendance look down on the footrace, and the man himself went away downcast and much humbler. Thus, Diogenes offered humanity no small service here: Whenever he saw someone putting on airs and going crazy over some worthless matter, he brought that person down to size a bit and removed a mote of ignorance, in the same way people prick and puncture swollen or inflated boils.

Ἐν δὲ τούτῳ θεασάμενος ἵππους ἐν τῷ αὐτῷ δεδεμένους, ἔπειτα μαχομένους τε καὶ λακτίζοντας αὐτούς, καὶ πολὺν ὄχλον περιεστῶτας καὶ θεωμένους, ἕως καμὼν ὁ ἕτερος ἔφυγεν ἀπορρήξας, προσελθὼν ἐστεφάνωσε τὸν μένοντα καὶ ἀνεκήρυττεν ὡς Ἰσθμιονίκην, ὅτι λακτίζων ἐνίκησεν. ἐπὶ τούτῳ γέλως καὶ θόρυβος ἦν ἁπάντων, καὶ τὸν Διογένη πολλοὶ ἐθαύμαζον καὶ τῶν ἀθλητῶν κατεγέλων, καί τινας ἀπελθεῖν φασιν οὐκ ἰδόντας αὐτούς,—ὅσοι κακῶς ἐσκήνουν ἢ καὶ τούτου ἠπόρουν.

On this same occasion, when Diogenes (with a large crowd standing around and watching) observed two horses tied together at the same hitch fighting and kicking each other until one, exhausted, broke away and fled, he walked up and crowned the horse who stayed behind and proclaimed for it an Isthmian prize because it had won at kicking. At this there was universal laughter and uproar. Many were in thrall to Diogenes and derided the athletes. They say, too, that some people left not having even watched the events—people whose tent-accommodation was poor, or who had no means to afford it.

8. Interview with a Cynic

(Pseudo-Lucian, *The Cynic*)

This anonymous dialogue, transmitted among the genuine works of Lucian of Samosata (see selection no. 5), is at once remarkable and mundane. On the one hand, it traffics in standard charges against Cynicism and tosses back many of the standard rebuttals. Its Ode to the Beard, for example, became a philosophic commonplace. (The emperor Julian wrote an entire invective against beard-haters.) What's remarkable, though, is the author's awareness of what economists now call "externalities," or the deleterious environmental side effects and human costs involved in the production and acquisition of goods. Relatedly, the Cynic interlocutor's preference for local products over items sourced from global trade rings even truer for our time. Both observations enlarge on the meaning of Cynic cosmopolitanism: The consequences of our choices, and thus our obligations to our environments and to one another, extend far and wide, and in many directions.

ΛΥΚΙΝΟΣ

Τί ποτε σύ, οὗτος, πώγωνα μὲν ἔχεις καὶ κόμην,
χιτῶνα δὲ οὐκ ἔχεις καὶ γυμνοδερκῇ καὶ
ἀνυποδητεῖς τὸν ἀλήτην καὶ ἀπάνθρωπον βίον
καὶ θηριώδη ἐπιλεξάμενος καὶ ἀεὶ τοῖς ἐνα-
ντίοις τὸ ἴδιον δέμας οὐχ ὡς οἱ πολλοὶ διαχρη-
σάμενος περινοστεῖς ἄλλοτε ἀλλαχοῦ, καὶ
εὐνηθησόμενος ἐπὶ ξηροῦ δαπέδου, ὡς ἄσην
πάμπολλον τὸ τριβώνιον φέρειν, οὐ μέντοι καὶ
τοῦτο λεπτὸν οὐδὲ μαλακὸν οὐδὲ ἀνθηρόν;

ΚΥΝΙΚΟΣ

Οὐδὲ γὰρ δέομαι· τοιοῦτον δὲ ὁποῖον ἂν
πορισθείη ῥᾷστα καὶ τῷ κτησαμένῳ πράγματα
ὡς ἐλάχιστα παρέχον· τοιοῦτον γὰρ ἀρκεῖ μοι.
σὺ δὲ πρὸς θεῶν εἰπέ μοι, τῇ πολυτελείᾳ οὐ
νομίζεις κακίαν προσεῖναι;

ΛΥΚΙΝΟΣ

Καὶ μάλα.

ΚΥΝΙΚΟΣ

Τῇ δὲ εὐτελείᾳ ἀρετήν;

INTERVIEW WITH A CYNIC

LYKINOS[1]

Hey, you there—you've got a beard and long hair, but why no shirt? Why do you show your nakedness and go around barefoot? Why have you chosen a vagrant, antisocial, animal-like lifestyle? You are constantly abusing your body with practices exactly opposite those of ordinary people. You wander about here and there looking to make your bed on the bare ground, which results in your cloak getting totally filthy (though, indeed, it was not delicate, soft, or fragrant to begin with). Why?

KYNIKOS

Well, I don't need one like that. This kind of cloak is the most easily sourced and offers the fewest hassles to the person who has acquired it. This kind suits me fine. But you, please, tell me: Do you not think that vice is connected to extravagance?

LYKINOS

Yes, I think it is.

KYNIKOS

And that virtue is connected to simplicity?

ΛΥΚΙΝΟΣ

Καὶ μάλα.

ΚΥΝΙΚΟΣ

Τί ποτε οὖν ὁρῶν ἐμὲ τῶν πολλῶν εὐτελέστε-
ρον διαιτώμενον, τοὺς δὲ πολυτελέστερον, ἐμὲ
αἰτιᾷ καὶ οὐκ ἐκείνους;

ΛΥΚΙΝΟΣ

Ὅτι οὐκ εὐτελέστερόν μοι, μὰ Δία, τῶν
πολλῶν διαιτᾶσθαι δοκεῖς, ἀλλ᾽ ἐνδεέστερον,
μᾶλλον δὲ τελέως ἐνδεῶς καὶ ἀπόρως· δια-
φέρεις γὰρ οὐδὲν σὺ τῶν πτωχῶν, οἳ τὴν
ἐφήμερον τροφὴν μεταιτοῦσιν.

ΚΥΝΙΚΟΣ

Βούλει οὖν ἴδωμεν, ἐπεὶ προελήλυθεν ἐνταῦθα
ὁ λόγος, τί τὸ ἐνδεὲς καὶ τί τὸ ἱκανόν ἐστιν;

ΛΥΚΙΝΟΣ

Εἴ σοι δοκεῖ.

INTERVIEW WITH A CYNIC

LYKINOS

Yes, indeed.

KYNIKOS

Then why, since you see me living more simply than ordinary people and them living more extravagantly, do you censure me and not them?

LYKINOS

Because you don't strike me as leading a life that is simpler than ordinary people, but one that is more *lacking*—nay, I swear, *completely* lacking and without recourse. You're no different than the beggars who mooch for their meals each day.

KYNIKOS

Well then, since the conversation has reached this topic, shall we examine what lack is and what sufficiency is? Are you willing to do that?

LYKINOS

If that seems best to you.

ΚΥΝΙΚΟΣ

Ἆρ᾽ οὖν ἱκανὸν μὲν ἑκάστῳ ὅπερ ἂν ἐξικνῆται
πρὸς τὴν ἐκείνου χρείαν, ἢ ἄλλο τι λέγεις;

ΛΥΚΙΝΟΣ

Ἔστω τοῦτο.

ΚΥΝΙΚΟΣ

Ἐνδεὲς δὲ ὅπερ ἂν ἐνδεέστερον ᾖ τῆς χρείας
καὶ μὴ ἐξικνῆται πρὸς τὸ δέον;

ΛΥΚΙΝΟΣ

Ναί.

ΚΥΝΙΚΟΣ

Οὐδὲν ἄρα τῶν ἐμῶν ἐνδεές ἐστιν· οὐδὲν γὰρ
αὐτῶν ὅ τι οὐ τὴν χρείαν ἐκτελεῖ τὴν ἐμήν.

ΛΥΚΙΝΟΣ

Πῶς τοῦτο λέγεις;

ΚΥΝΙΚΟΣ

Ἐὰν σκοπῇς πρὸς ὅ τι γέγονεν ἕκαστον ὧν
δεόμεθα, οἷον οἰκία ἆρ᾽ οὐχὶ σκέπης;

KYNIKOS

Isn't what suffices for each person precisely
what meets that person's needs? Or would
you say something different?

LYKINOS

No, I would agree with that.

KYNIKOS

And isn't lack precisely that which falls short
and doesn't meet the need it should?

LYKINOS

Yes.

KYNIKOS

Then there's nothing lacking in my affairs.
Nothing in my lifestyle fails to accomplish its
end, as far as my needs go.

LYKINOS

How do you mean?

KYNIKOS

If you consider the purpose of something we
need, say, a house: Doesn't a house exist
because we need protection?

ΛΥΚΙΝΟΣ
 Ναί.

ΚΥΝΙΚΟΣ
 Τί δέ; ἐσθὴς τοῦ χάριν; ἆρα οὐχὶ καὶ αὕτη τῆς σκέπης;

ΛΥΚΙΝΟΣ
 Ναί.

ΚΥΝΙΚΟΣ
 Τῆς δὲ σκέπης αὐτῆς πρὸς θεῶν τίνος ἐδεήθημεν ἕνεκα; οὐχ ὥστε ἄμεινον ἔχειν τὸν σκεπόμενον;

ΛΥΚΙΝΟΣ
 Δοκεῖ μοι.

ΚΥΝΙΚΟΣ
 Πότερ' οὖν τὼ πόδε κάκιον ἔχειν δοκῶ σοι;

ΛΥΚΙΝΟΣ
 Οὐκ οἶδα.

ΚΥΝΙΚΟΣ
 Ἀλλ' οὕτως ἂν μάθοις· τί ποδῶν ἔστ' ἔργον;

ΛΥΚΙΝΟΣ
 Πορεύεσθαι.

LYKINOS

Yes.

KYNIKOS

OK, so what are clothes for? Do they not also satisfy our need for protection?

LYKINOS

Yes.

KYNIKOS

But what about protection itself, if I may ask? What need have we of it? Is it not so that the one protected is kept in a better state?

LYKINOS

Seems so.

KYNIKOS

Do my feet seem inferior to you?

LYKINOS

I have no idea.

KYNIKOS

Well, learn the answer as follows. What is the function of feet?

LYKINOS

To walk.

ΚΥΝΙΚΟΣ

Κάκιον οὖν πορεύεσθαί σοι δοκοῦσιν οἱ ἐμοὶ
πόδες ἢ οἱ τῶν πολλῶν;

ΛΥΚΙΝΟΣ

Τοῦτο μὲν οὐκ ἴσως.

ΚΥΝΙΚΟΣ

Οὐ τοίνυν οὐδὲ χεῖρον ἔχουσιν, εἰ μὴ χεῖρον τὸ
ἑαυτῶν ἔργον ἀποδιδόασιν.

ΛΥΚΙΝΟΣ

Ἴσως.

ΚΥΝΙΚΟΣ

Τοὺς μὲν δὴ πόδας οὐδὲν φαίνομαι χεῖρον
διακείμενος τῶν πολλῶν ἔχειν.

ΛΥΚΙΝΟΣ

Οὐκ ἔοικας.

ΚΥΝΙΚΟΣ

Τί δέ; τοὐμὸν σῶμα τὸ λοιπὸν ἆρα κάκιον; εἰ
γὰρ κάκιον, καὶ ἀσθενέστερον, ἀρετὴ γὰρ
σώματος ἰσχύς. ἆρ᾽ οὖν τὸ ἐμὸν ἀσθενέστερον;

ΛΥΚΙΝΟΣ

Οὐ φαίνεται.

KYNIKOS

Do my feet strike you as worse at walking
than ordinary people's?

LYKINOS

In that respect, probably no.

KYNIKOS

Then they're not inferior, if they fulfill their
function no worse.

LYKINOS

Perhaps.

KYNIKOS

So, with respect to feet, I appear no worse off
than ordinary people.

LYKINOS

I guess you don't.

KYNIKOS

OK then, consider the rest of my body: Is it
inferior? For if it's inferior it's also weaker, for
the excellence of the body consists in strength.
Is mine weaker?

LYKINOS

It doesn't appear to be.

ΚΥΝΙΚΟΣ

Οὐ τοίνυν οὔθ᾽ οἱ πόδες φαίνοιντό μοι σκέπης
ἐνδεῶς ἔχειν οὔτε τὸ λοιπὸν σῶμα· εἰ γὰρ ἐνδεῶς
εἶχον, κακῶς ἂν εἶχον. ἡ γὰρ ἔνδεια πανταχοῦ
κακὸν καὶ χεῖρον ἔχειν ποιεῖ ταῦτα οἷς ἂν προσῇ.
ἀλλὰ μὴν οὐδὲ τρέφεσθαί γε φαίνεται χεῖρον τὸ
σῶμα τοὐμόν, ὅτι ἀπὸ τῶν τυχόντων τρέφεται.

ΛΥΚΙΝΟΣ

Δῆλον γάρ.

ΚΥΝΙΚΟΣ

Οὐδὲ εὔρωστον, εἰ κακῶς ἐτρέφετο· λυμαίνονται γὰρ αἱ πονηραὶ τροφαὶ τὰ σώματα.

ΛΥΚΙΝΟΣ

Ἔστι ταῦτα.

ΚΥΝΙΚΟΣ

Τί ποτ᾽ οὖν, εἰπέ μοι, τούτων οὕτως ἐχόντων
αἰτιᾷ μου καὶ φαυλίζεις τὸν βίον καὶ φὴς
ἄθλιον;

ΛΥΚΙΝΟΣ

Ὅτι, νὴ Δία, τῆς φύσεως, ἣν σὺ τιμᾷς, καὶ τῶν
θεῶν γῆν ἐν μέσῳ κατατεθεικότων, ἐκ δὲ αὐτῆς

KYNIKOS

Then neither my feet nor my body would appear to be lacking in protection, for if they were lacking, they would be in poor condition. For lack is a bad thing wherever it occurs and makes what is associated with it to be in worse condition. Also, no worse *nourished* does my body appear to be either for getting its sustenance from whatever food I happen upon.

LYKINOS

That's clear.

KYNIKOS

It wouldn't be strong if it were poorly nourished, for bad food harms bodies.

LYKINOS

True enough.

KYNIKOS

So, tell me, then, why on earth, since all these things are so, do you censure me and belittle my lifestyle and say it's miserable?

LYKINOS

Because, honestly, although Nature, which you revere, and the gods created the Earth for

ἀναδεδωκότων πολλὰ κἀγαθά, ὥστε ἔχειν ἡμᾶς
πάντα ἄφθονα μὴ πρὸς τὴν χρείαν μόνον, ἀλλὰ
καὶ πρὸς ἡδονήν, σὺ πάντων τούτων ἢ τῶν γε
πλείστων ἄμοιρος εἶ καὶ οὐδενὸς μετέχεις
αὐτῶν οὐδὲν μᾶλλον ἢ τὰ θηρία· πίνεις μὲν γὰρ
ὕδωρ ὅπερ καὶ τὰ θηρία, σιτῇ δὲ ὅπερ ἂν εὑρί-
σκῃς, ὥσπερ οἱ κύνες, εὐνὴν δὲ οὐδὲν κρείττω
τῶν κυνῶν ἔχεις· χόρτος γὰρ ἀρκεῖ σοι καθάπερ ἐκείνοις. ἔτι δὲ ἱμάτιον φορεῖς οὐδὲν
ἐπιεικέστερον ἀκλήρου. καίτοι εἰ σὺ τούτοις
ἀρκούμενος ὀρθῶς φρονήσεις, ὁ θεὸς οὐκ
ὀρθῶς ἐποίησε τοῦτο μὲν πρόβατα ποιήσας
ἔμμαλλα, τοῦτο δ' ἀμπέλους ἡδυοίνους, τοῦτο
δὲ τὴν ἄλλην παρασκευὴν θαυμαστῶς ποικίλην
καὶ ἔλαιον καὶ μέλι καὶ τὰ ἄλλα, ὡς ἔχειν μὲν
ἡμᾶς σιτία παντοδαπά, ἔχειν δὲ ποτὸν ἡδύ,
ἔχειν δὲ χρήματα, ἔχειν δὲ εὐνὴν μαλακήν,
ἔχειν δὲ οἰκίας καλὰς καὶ τὰ ἄλλα πάντα
θαυμαστῶς κατεσκευασμένα· καὶ γὰρ οὔ τὰ
τῶν τεχνῶν ἔργα δῶρα τῶν θεῶν ἐστι. τὸ δὲ
πάντων τούτων ζῆν ἀπεστερημένον ἄθλιον
μέν, εἰ καὶ ὑπὸ ἄλλου τινὸς ἀπεστέρητο καθάπερ οἱ ἐν τοῖς δεσμωτηρίοις· πολὺ δὲ ἀθλιώτε-
ρον, εἴ τις αὐτὸς ἑαυτὸν ἀποστεροίη πάντων

the common weal and have sent up from it
good things in abundance for us to use, not
only for our needs, but also for our pleasure,
you take no part in any of these things, or
almost none, and engage with them no more
than animals do. You drink water like an
animal. You eat whatever you find, as do dogs.
Your bed is no better than a dog's. A manger
suits you as suits them. What is more, the
cloak you wear is no nicer than a destitute
person's. However, if you are right in thinking
to be content with these conditions, the god
was not right to have given sheep fleeces, or to
have made vines that produce sweet wine, or
to have rendered other products dazzlingly
varied, like olives and honey and the rest,
whose purpose is so that we have foods of
every type, and sweet drink, and money, and a
soft bed, and beautiful houses, and all our
other furnishings wondrously provided. The
works of the arts are also the gods' gifts. To
live bereft of all these things is miserable, even
if one has been deprived of them by some
other means, as is the case with prisoners. But
it's much more miserable if someone deprives

τῶν καλῶν, μανία ἤδη τοῦτό γε σαφής.

ΚΥΝΙΚΟΣ
Ἀλλ᾽ ἴσως ὀρθῶς λέγεις. ἐκεῖνο δέ μοι εἰπέ, εἴ
τις ἀνδρὸς πλουσίου προθύμως καὶ φιλο-
φρόνως ἑστιῶντος καὶ ξενίζοντος πολλοὺς ἅμα
καὶ παντοδαπούς, τοὺς μὲν ἀσθενεῖς, τοὺς δὲ
ἐρρωμένους, κἄπειτα παραθέντος πολλὰ καὶ
παντοδαπά, πάντα ἁρπάζοι καὶ πάντα ἐσθίοι,
μὴ τὰ πλησίον μόνον, ἀλλὰ καὶ τὰ πόρρω τὰ
τοῖς ἀσθενοῦσι παρεσκευασμένα ὑγιαίνων
αὐτός, καὶ ταῦτα μίαν μὲν κοιλίαν ἔχων,
ὀλίγων δὲ ὥστε τραφῆναι δεόμενος, ὑπὸ τῶν
πολλῶν ἐπιτριβήσεσθαι μέλλων, οὗτος ὁ ἀνὴρ
ποῖός τις δοκεῖ σοι εἶναι; ἆρά γε φρόνιμος;

ΛΥΚΙΝΟΣ
Οὐκ ἔμοιγε.

ΚΥΝΙΚΟΣ
Τί δέ; σώφρων;

ΛΥΚΙΝΟΣ
Οὐδὲ τοῦτο.

himself of all these good things. Indeed, that is plain madness.

KYNIKOS

Well, maybe you're right. But tell me this: If a rich man holds a feast and shows himself to be a kind and generous host by inviting all sorts of people to it, both the weak and the strong, then, after he has set out all sorts of dishes, a guest were to snatch up and eat everything, not only what was near to him but also food that was far from his reach—food provisioned for the ailing, even though he himself is healthy, and has, what is more, only one stomach anyhow so needs only a little to be fed and will ruin himself by eating so much— what do you make of such a person? Is he sensible?

LYKINOS

No, not in my opinion.

KYNIKOS

Is he moderate?

LYKINOS

Not that either.

ΚΥΝΙΚΟΣ

Τί δέ; εἴ τις μετέχων τῆς αὐτῆς ταύτης τραπέ-
ζης τῶν μὲν πολλῶν καὶ ποικίλων ἀμελεῖ, ἓν δὲ
τῶν ἔγγιστα κειμένων ἐπιλεξάμενος, ἱκανῶς
ἔχον πρὸς τὴν ἑαυτοῦ χρείαν, τοῦτο ἐσθίοι
κοσμίως καὶ τούτῳ μόνῳ χρῷτο, τοῖς δὲ ἄλλοις
οὐδὲ προσβλέποι, τοῦτον οὐχ ἡγῇ σωφρονέ-
στερον καὶ ἀμείνω ἄνδρα ἐκείνου;

ΛΥΚΙΝΟΣ

Ἔγωγε.

ΚΥΝΙΚΟΣ

Πότερον οὖν συνίης, ἢ ἐμὲ δεῖ λέγειν;

ΛΥΚΙΝΟΣ

Τὸ ποῖον;

ΚΥΝΙΚΟΣ

Ὅτι ὁ μὲν θεὸς τῷ ξενίζοντι καλῶς ἐκείνῳ
ἔοικε παρατιθεὶς πολλὰ καὶ ποικίλα καὶ παντοδαπά, ὅπως ἔχωσιν ἁρμόζοντα, τὰ μὲν ὑγιαί-
νουσι, τὰ δὲ νοσοῦσι, καὶ τὰ μὲν ἰσχυροῖς, τὰ δὲ
ἀσθενοῦσιν, οὐχ ἵνα χρώμεθα ἅπασι πάντες,
ἀλλ᾽ ἵνα τοῖς καθ᾽ ἑαυτὸν ἕκαστος καὶ τῶν καθ᾽
ἑαυτὸν ὅτουπερ ἂν τύχῃ μάλιστα δεόμενος.

KYNIKOS

Alternatively, if someone sharing the same table is uninterested in the variety of many dishes but chooses the dish lying closest to him as sufficient for his own need and eats this in an orderly fashion, enjoying this dish only and not even looking at the others, do you not consider him more moderate and a better person than the other man?

LYKINOS

I do.

KYNIKOS

So, do you get it, or must I explain?

LYKINOS

Get what?

KYNIKOS

That god is like the good host: He places before us a variety of many kinds of dishes so that we have what is appropriate for us—some things for the healthy, some for the sick, some for the strong, some for the weak—not so that we all may use everything, but so that each of us might use for ourselves what falls in our

ὑμεῖς δὲ τῷ δι᾿ ἀπληστίαν τε καὶ ἀκρασίαν
ἁρπάζοντι πάντα τούτῳ μάλιστα ἐοίκατε πᾶσι
χρῆσθαι ἀξιοῦντες καὶ τοῖς ἀπανταχοῦ, μὴ τοῖς
παρ᾿ ὑμῖν μόνον, οὐ γῆν οὐ θάλατταν τὴν καθ᾿
αὑτοὺς αὐταρκεῖν νομίζοντες, ἀλλ᾿ ἀπὸ
περάτων γῆς ἐμπορευόμενοι τὰς ἡδονὰς καὶ τὰ
ξενικὰ τῶν ἐπιχωρίων ἀεὶ προτιμῶντες καὶ τὰ
πολυτελῆ τῶν εὐτελῶν καὶ τὰ δυσπόριστα τῶν
εὐπορίστων, καθόλου δὲ πράγματα καὶ κακὰ
ἔχειν μᾶλλον ἐθέλοντες ἢ ἄνευ πραγμάτων ζῆν·
τὰ γὰρ δὴ πολλὰ καὶ τίμια καὶ εὐδαιμονικὰ
παρασκευάσματα, ἐφ᾿ οἷς ἀγάλλεσθε, διὰ
πολλῆς ὑμῖν ταῦτα κακοδαιμονίας καὶ ταλαιπω-
ρίας παραγίγνεται. σκόπει γὰρ, εἰ βούλει, τὸν
πολύευκτον χρυσόν, σκόπει τὸν ἄργυρον,
σκόπει τὰς οἰκίας τὰς πολυτελεῖς, σκόπει τὰς
ἐσθῆτας τὰς ἐσπουδασμένας, σκόπει τὰ
τούτοις ἀκόλουθα πάντα, πόσων πραγμάτων
ἐστὶν ὤνια, πόσων πόνων, πόσων κινδύνων,
μᾶλλον δὲ αἵματος καὶ θανάτου καὶ διαφθορᾶς
ἀνθρώπων πόσης, οὐ μόνον ὅτι πλέοντες
ἀπόλλυνται διὰ ταῦτα πολλοὶ καὶ ζητοῦντες καὶ
δημιουργοῦντες δεινὰ πάσχουσιν, ἀλλ᾿ ὅτι καὶ
πολυμάχητά ἐστι καὶ ἐπιβουλεύετε ἀλλήλοις
διὰ ταῦτα καὶ φίλοις φίλοι καὶ πατράσι παῖδες
καὶ γυναῖκες ἀνδράσιν. οὕτως οἶμαι καὶ τὴν

domain and, of those things, what we happen
to need most.

Whereas you[2] are very much like that
person who grabs everything out of greed and
lack of restraint. You think it's fine to use it
all, including goods from all over and not just
what you have close to hand. You don't think
your own land and sea are enough in themselves but import your pleasures from the
corners of the globe and always prefer what is
foreign to what is produced locally, what is
costly to what is inexpensive, and what's hard
to procure to what's easily acquired. In short,
you prefer to have trouble and woe to living
without troubles, for the many costly goods
you think conducive to your happiness, over
which you exult, only come to be yours
through misery and suffering. Think about
the gold you pray so hard to get your hands
on, the silver, the expensive houses, the finely
tailored clothing, and all the accoutrements
that go along with these things: How much do
they cost in trouble? How much in human
labor and danger, or rather, in human blood,
death, and destruction? Not only because
many people are lost at sea for the sake of

Ἐριφύλην διὰ τὸν χρυσὸν προδοῦναι τὸν ἄνδρα.

καὶ ταῦτα μέντοι πάντα γίνεται, τῶν τε ποικίλων ἱματίων οὐδέν τι μᾶλλον θάλπειν δυναμένων, τῶν δὲ χρυσορόφων οἰκιῶν οὐδέν τι μᾶλλον σκεπουσῶν, τῶν δὲ ἐκπωμάτων τῶν ἀργυρῶν οὐκ ὠφελούντων τὸν πότον οὐδὲ τῶν χρυσῶν, οὐδ' αὖ τῶν ἐλεφαντίνων κλινῶν τὸν ὕπνον ἡδίω παρεχομένων, ἀλλ' ὄψει πολλάκις ἐπὶ τῆς ἐλεφαντίνης κλίνης καὶ τῶν πολυτελῶν στρωμάτων τοὺς εὐδαίμονας ὕπνου λαχεῖν οὐ δυναμένους. ὅτι μὲν γὰρ αἱ παντοδαπαὶ περὶ τὰ βρώματα πραγματεῖαι τρέφουσι μὲν οὐδὲν μᾶλλον, λυμαίνονται δὲ τὰ σώματα καὶ τοῖς σώμασι νόσους ἐμποιοῦσι, τί δεῖ λέγειν;

τί δὲ καὶ λέγειν, ὅσα τῶν ἀφροδισίων ἕνεκα πράγματα ποιοῦσί τε καὶ πάσχουσιν οἱ ἄνθρω-ποι; καίτοι ῥᾴδιον θεραπεύειν ταύτην τὴν

these things and the people who search them out or manufacture them suffer terribly, but also because these items are much fought over. You plot against one another to acquire them— friends against friends, sons against fathers, wives against husbands. Thus it was, I take it, that Eriphyle betrayed her husband for gold.[3]

All this takes place, and yet embroidered robes can keep you no warmer, gilt houses cannot provide more shelter, cups of gold and silver don't help the taste of drink, nor do beds carved from ivory offer you a sounder sleep. To the contrary, you will often see the well-off lying upon an ivory bed with expensive sheets unable to get a wink of sleep. And not only does elaborate fuss over preparation of food not nourish you better, but such cuisine harms bodies and causes disease. Need I mention that?

And need I also mention all the trouble people cause and suffer in pursuit of sex? Yet it's easy to service that urge—unless one opts for

ἐπιθυμίαν, εἰ μή τις ἐθέλοι τρυφᾶν. καὶ οὐδ᾽ εἰς
ταύτην ἡ μανία καὶ διαφθορὰ φαίνεται τοῖς
ἀνθρώποις ἀρκεῖν, ἀλλ᾽ ἤδη καὶ τῶν ὄντων τὴν
χρῆσιν ἀναστρέφουσιν ἑκάστῳ χρώμενοι πρὸς
ὃ μὴ πέφυκεν, ὥσπερ εἴ τις ἀνθ᾽ ἁμάξης ἐθέλοι
τῇ κλίνῃ καθάπερ ἁμάξῃ χρήσασθαι.

ΛΥΚΙΝΟΣ
Καὶ τίς οὗτος;

ΚΥΝΙΚΟΣ
Ὑμεῖς, οἳ τοῖς ἀνθρώποις ἅτε ὑποζυγίοις
χρῆσθε, κελεύετε δὲ αὐτοὺς ὥσπερ ἁμάξας τὰς
κλίνας τοῖς τραχήλοις ἄγειν, αὐτοὶ δ᾽ ἄνω
κατάκεισθε τρυφῶντες καὶ ἐκεῖθεν ὥσπερ
ὄνους ἡνιοχεῖτε τοὺς ἀνθρώπους ταύτην, ἀλλὰ
μὴ ταύτην τρέπεσθαι κελεύοντες· καὶ οἱ ταῦτα
μάλιστα ποιοῦντες μάλιστα μακαρίζεσθε. οἱ δὲ
τοῖς κρέασι μὴ τροφῇ χρώμενοι μόνον, ἀλλὰ
καὶ βαφὰς μηχανώμενοι δι᾽ αὐτῶν, οἷοί γέ εἰσιν
οἱ τὴν πορφύραν βάπτοντες, οὐχὶ καὶ αὐτοὶ
παρὰ φύσιν χρῶνται τοῖς τοῦ θεοῦ
κατασκευάσμασιν;

ΛΥΚΙΝΟΣ
Νὴ Δία· δύναται γὰρ βάπτειν, οὐκ ἐσθίεσθαι
μόνον τὸ τῆς πορφύρας κρέας.

extravagance. When it comes to sex, not even derangement and corruption seem to be enough for people, but these days they pervert the proper use of what's out there, using each thing contrary to its natural purpose, as if someone were to opt to use a bed for a wagon.[4]

LYKINOS
And who does that?

KYNIKOS
You do! You use people like yoked animals to carry your daybeds on their necks as if they were wagons while you yourselves lie back, luxuriate, and from that position steer human beings as if they were donkeys, ordering them to turn this way rather than that, and the more you do this the more fortunate you feel. Similarly, you use flesh not only for food, but to fabricate dyes as well, as, for example, with those who dye cloth purple.[5] Do you not think they abuse god's creation, contrary to Nature?

LYKINOS
No, by Zeus, I do not. For one can both eat the flesh of a mussel and use it as a dye.

ΚΥΝΙΚΟΣ

Ἀλλ' οὐ πρὸς τοῦτο γέγονεν· ἐπεὶ καὶ τῷ
κρατῆρι δύναιτ' ἄν τις βιαζόμενος ὥσπερ
χύτρᾳ χρήσασθαι, πλὴν οὐ πρὸς τοῦτο γέγονεν.
ἀλλὰ γὰρ πῶς ἅπασαν τὴν τούτων τις κακοδαιμονίαν διελθεῖν δύναιτ' ἄν; τοσαύτη τίς ἐστι.
σὺ δέ μοι, διότι μὴ βούλομαι ταύτης μετέχειν,
ἐγκαλεῖς· ζῶ δὲ καθάπερ ὁ κόσμιος ἐκεῖνος,
εὐωχούμενος τοῖς κατ' ἐμαυτὸν καὶ τοῖς
εὐτελεστάτοις χρώμενος, τῶν δὲ ποικίλων καὶ
παντοδαπῶν οὐκ ἐφιέμενος.

κἄπειτα εἰ θηρίου βίον βραχέων δεόμενος
καὶ ὀλίγοις χρώμενος δοκῶ σοι ζῆν, κινδυ-
νεύουσιν οἱ θεοὶ καὶ τῶν θηρίων εἶναι χείρονες
κατά γε τὸν σὸν λόγον· οὐδενὸς γὰρ δέονται.
ἵνα δὲ καταμάθῃς ἀκριβέστερον τό τε ὀλίγων
καὶ τὸ πολλῶν δεῖσθαι ποῖόν τι ἑκάτερόν ἐστιν,
ἐννόησον ὅτι δέονται πλειόνων οἱ μὲν παῖδες
τῶν τελείων, αἱ δὲ γυναῖκες τῶν ἀνδρῶν, οἱ δὲ
νοσοῦντες τῶν ὑγιαινόντων, καθόλου δὲ
πανταχοῦ τὸ χεῖρον τοῦ κρείττονος πλειόνων
δεῖται. διὰ τοῦτο θεοὶ μὲν οὐδενός, οἱ δὲ
ἔγγιστα θεοῖς ἐλαχίστων δέονται.

ἢ νομίζεις τὸν Ἡρακλέα τὸν πάντων
ἀνθρώπων ἄριστον, θεῖον δὲ ἄνδρα καὶ θεὸν
ὀρθῶς νομισθέντα, διὰ κακοδαιμονίαν περινο-

INTERVIEW WITH A CYNIC

KYNIKOS

But it wasn't created for that purpose. So, too, someone could compel a mixing bowl for wine to be used as a pitcher, except that's not what it was devised for. In any event, how could one ever recount all the wretchedness caused by such practices? Some of it is considerable. And yet you indict me because I refuse to have anything to do with it? Actually, I live like that orderly person feasting on what falls in my domain and consuming what is least expensive. I don't crave commodities of intricate variety.

Moreover, if you think I live the life of an animal because my needs are few and I use but little, perhaps the gods are inferior even to the animals according to your logic, for the gods need nothing. What is more, so that you may learn what needing little is versus needing much, note that children need more than adults, women more than men, the diseased more than the healthy—in sum, in every case what is worse is more needy than what is better. Consequently, the gods need nothing and those closest to the gods need next to nothing.

στεῖν γυμνὸν δέρμα μόνον ἔχοντα καὶ μηδενὸς
τῶν αὐτῶν ὑμῖν δεόμενον; ἀλλ᾽ οὐ κακοδαίμων
ἦν ἐκεῖνος, ὃς καὶ τῶν ἄλλων ἀπήμυνε τὰ κακά,
οὐδ᾽ αὖ πένης, ὃς γῆς καὶ θαλάττης ἦρχεν· ἐφ᾽
ὅ τι γὰρ ὁρμήσειεν, ἁπανταχοῦ πάντων ἐκράτει
καὶ οὐδενὶ τῶν τότε ἐνέτυχεν ὁμοίῳ οὐδὲ
κρείττονι ἑαυτοῦ, μέχριπερ ἐξ ἀνθρώπων
ἀπῆλθεν. ἢ σὺ δοκεῖς στρωμάτων καὶ ὑποδη-
μάτων ἀπόρως ἔχειν καὶ διὰ τοῦτο περιιέναι
τοιοῦτον; οὐκ ἔστιν εἰπεῖν, ἀλλ᾽ ἐγκρατὴς καὶ
καρτερικὸς ἦν καὶ κρατεῖν ἤθελε καὶ τρυφᾶν
οὐκ ἐβούλετο.

ὁ δὲ Θησεὺς ὁ τούτου μαθητὴς οὐ βασιλεὺς
μὲν ἦν πάντων Ἀθηναίων, υἱὸς δὲ Ποσειδῶνος,
ὥς φασιν, ἄριστος δὲ τῶν καθ᾽ αὑτόν; ἀλλ᾽
ὅμως κἀκεῖνος ἤθελεν ἀνυπόδητος εἶναι καὶ
γυμνὸς βαδίζειν καὶ πώγωνα καὶ κόμην ἔχειν
ἤρεσκεν αὐτῷ, καὶ οὐκ ἐκείνῳ μόνῳ, ἀλλὰ καὶ
πᾶσι τοῖς παλαιοῖς ἤρεσκεν· ἀμείνους γὰρ ἦσαν
ὑμῶν, καὶ οὐκ ἂν ὑπέμειναν οὐδὲ εἷς αὐτῶν
οὐδὲν μᾶλλον ἢ τῶν λεόντων τις ξυρώμενος·

Do you think that Heracles, the best of all human beings, a godlike man and rightly reckoned a god himself, wandered around naked, wearing only an animal skin and in need of none of the things that you possess because he was unfortunate? No, he was not unfortunate. He protected others from wrong. Nor was he poor, as he held sway over land and sea. Whatever he set his hand to he conquered—everything, everywhere—and never met anyone who was his equal or superior until he parted company with the human race. Do you think he went around as he did because he was at a loss for acquiring blankets or sandals? No, one couldn't say that about him, since he was self-disciplined and full of endurance. He wanted to be in control, not to luxuriate.

And what about Theseus, his pupil? Was he not king over all the Athenians—Poseidon's son they say—and the best man of his generation? Nevertheless, he too chose to walk about naked and unshod, and wearing a beard and long hair suited him just fine,[6] and not him only, but all the ancients. They were assuredly

ὑγρότητα γὰρ καὶ λειότητα σαρκὸς γυναιξὶ
πρέπειν ἡγοῦντο, αὐτοὶ δ' ὥσπερ ἦσαν, καὶ
φαίνεσθαι ἄνδρες ἤθελον καὶ τὸν πώγωνα
κόσμον ἀνδρὸς ἐνόμιζον ὥσπερ καὶ ἵππων
χαίτην καὶ λεόντων γένεια, οἷς ὁ θεὸς ἀγλαΐας
καὶ κόσμου χάριν προσέθηκέ τινα· οὑτωσὶ δὲ
καὶ τοῖς ἀνδράσι τὸν πώγωνα προσέθηκεν.
ἐκείνους οὖν ἐγὼ ζηλῶ τοὺς παλαιοὺς καὶ
ἐκείνους μιμεῖσθαι βούλομαι, τοὺς δὲ νῦν οὐ
ζηλῶ τῆς θαυμαστῆς ταύτης εὐδαιμονίας ἣν
ἔχουσι καὶ περὶ τραπέζας καὶ ἐσθῆτας καὶ
λεαίνοντες καὶ ψιλούμενοι πᾶν τοῦ σώματος
μέρος καὶ μηδὲ τῶν ἀπορρήτων μηδέν, ᾗ
πέφυκεν, ἔχειν ἐῶντες.

  εὔχομαι δέ μοι τοὺς μὲν πόδας ὁπλῶν ἱππείων
οὐδὲν διαφέρειν, ὥσπερ φασὶ τοὺς Χείρωνος,
αὐτὸς δὲ μὴ δεῖσθαι στρωμάτων ὥσπερ οἱ
λέοντες, οὐδὲ τροφῆς δεῖσθαι πολυτελοῦς
μᾶλλον ἢ οἱ κύνες· εἴη δέ μοι γῆν μὲν ἅπασαν

better men than you, yet they would no sooner submit to being shaved than would a lion. They thought soft and smooth skin suited women, but since they were men, they wished to look like men. They reckoned a beard was a man's adornment as a mane is for a horse and a lion, to whom the god has given certain attributes as their glory and adornment. That's why the god gave men a beard and I therefore admire the men of old and wish to imitate them. I do *not* admire those who enjoy what they consider their amazing fortune when it comes to food and fashion: They polish themselves by depilating every part of their bodies, not even keeping their private parts in the state that Nature intended.

As for me, I pray for feet no different from horses' hooves, as they say Chiron had,[7] and, like lions, not to need bedding, and, like dogs, not to require expensive food. May I have the whole Earth for a bed that is sufficient in itself. May I consider the universe my home. May I choose for food what is easiest to obtain. Gold and silver, may I, and my friends,

εὐνὴν αὐτάρκη ἔχειν, οἶκον δὲ τὸν κόσμον
νομίζειν, τροφὴν δὲ αἱρεῖσθαι τὴν ῥάστην
πορισθῆναι. χρυσοῦ δὲ καὶ ἀργύρου μὴ δεη-
θείην μήτ᾽ οὖν ἐγὼ μήτε τῶν ἐμῶν φίλων
μηδείς· πάντα γὰρ τὰ κακὰ τοῖς ἀνθρώποις ἐκ
τῆς τούτων ἐπιθυμίας φύονται, καὶ στάσεις καὶ
πόλεμοι καὶ ἐπιβουλαὶ καὶ σφαγαί. ταυτὶ πάντα
πηγὴν ἔχει τὴν ἐπιθυμίαν τοῦ πλείονος· ἀλλ᾽
ἡμῶν αὕτη ἀπείη, καὶ πλεονεξίας μήποτε
ὀρεχθείην, μειονεκτῶν δ᾽ ἀνέχεσθαι δυναίμην.

τοιαῦτά σοι τά γε ἡμέτερα, πολὺ δήπου
διάφωνα τοῖς τῶν πολλῶν βουλήμασι· καὶ
θαυμαστὸν οὐδέν, εἰ τῷ σχήματι διαφέρομεν
αὐτῶν, ὁπότε καὶ τῇ προαιρέσει τοσοῦτον
διαφέρομεν. θαυμάζω δέ σου πῶς ποτε κι-
θαρῳδοῦ μέν τινα νομίζεις στολὴν καὶ σχῆμα,
καὶ αὐλητοῦ νὴ Δία σχῆμα, καὶ στολὴν τραγῳ-
δοῦ, ἀνδρὸς δὲ ἀγαθοῦ σχῆμα καὶ στολὴν
οὐκέτι νομίζεις, ἀλλὰ τὴν αὐτὴν αὐτὸν οἴει δεῖν
ἔχειν τοῖς πολλοῖς, καὶ ταῦτα τῶν πολλῶν κακῶν
ὄντων. εἰ μὲν δεῖ ἑνὸς ἰδίου σχήματος τοῖς
ἀγαθοῖς, τί πρέποι ἂν μᾶλλον ἢ τοῦθ᾽ ὅπερ
ἀναιδέστατον τοῖς ἀκολάστοις ἐστὶ καὶ ὅπερ
ἀπεύξαιντ᾽ ἂν οὗτοι μάλιστα ἔχειν;

need none. All human woes spring from desire
for it—civic conflicts, wars, conspiracies, and
slaughter. All these things have their source in
the desire for more. May that desire be far
from us. May I never overreach to grab more.
Indeed, may I be able to cope with having less.

These, let me assure you, are *our* priorities.
They are, of course, discordant with the wishes
of ordinary people. No wonder that we differ
from them in dress when we are so different in
our purpose. I'm surprised at you, though,
how you acknowledge that a lyre-player
wears a particular cloak and costume, as does
a shawm-player and a tragic actor, but you don't
yet acknowledge that a good man has his cloak
and costume too. You think he should wear the
same garb as ordinary people, in spite of the fact
that ordinary people are wicked. If good people
need their own costume particular to them, what
would be more appropriate than this, which
seems shameless to the indulgent and which they
themselves would loathe to wear.

Accordingly, this is the kind of garb I wear—
it's rough, it's shaggy, I wear an old cloak, have
long hair, and my feet are bare—whereas

οὐκοῦν τό γε ἐμὸν σχῆμα τοιοῦτόν ἐστιν,
αὐχμηρὸν εἶναι, λάσιον εἶναι, τρίβωνα ἔχειν,
κομᾶν, ἀνυποδητεῖν, τὸ δ᾽ ὑμέτερον ὅμοιον τῷ
τῶν κιναίδων, καὶ διακρίνειν οὐδὲ εἷς ἂν ἔχοι,
οὐ τῇ χροιᾷ τῶν ἱματίων, οὐ τῇ μαλακότητι, οὐ
τῷ πλήθει τῶν χιτωνίσκων, οὐ τοῖς ἀμφιέσμα-
σιν, οὐχ ὑποδήμασιν, οὐ κατασκευῇ τριχῶν, οὐκ
ὀδμῇ· καὶ γὰρ καὶ ἀπόζετε ἤδη παραπλήσιον
ἐκείνοις οἱ εὐδαιμονέστατοι οὗτοι μάλιστα.
καίτοι τί ἂν δῴη τις ἀνδρὸς τὴν αὐτὴν τοῖς
κιναίδοις ὀδμὴν ἔχοντος; τοιγαροῦν τοὺς μὲν
πόνους οὐδὲν ἐκείνων μᾶλλον ἀνέχεσθε, τὰς δὲ
ἡδονὰς οὐδὲν ἐκείνων ἧττον· καὶ τρέφεσθε τοῖς
αὐτοῖς καὶ κοιμᾶσθε ὁμοίως καὶ βαδίζετε,
μᾶλλον δὲ βαδίζειν οὐκ ἐθέλετε, φέρεσθε δὲ
ὥσπερ τὰ φορτία οἱ μὲν ὑπ᾽ ἀνθρώπων, οἱ δὲ
ὑπὸ κτηνῶν· ἐμὲ δὲ οἱ πόδες φέρουσιν ὅποιπερ
ἂν δέωμαι. κἀγὼ μὲν ἱκανὸς καὶ ῥίγους ἀνέχεσθαι καὶ θάλπος φέρειν καὶ τοῖς τῶν θεῶν
ἔργοις μὴ δυσχεραίνειν, διότι ἄθλιός εἰμι, ὑμεῖς
δὲ διὰ τὴν εὐδαιμονίαν οὐδενὶ τῶν γινομένων
ἀρέσκεσθε καὶ πάντα μέμφεσθε καὶ τὰ μὲν
παρόντα φέρειν οὐκ ἐθέλετε, τῶν δὲ ἀπόντων
ἐφίεσθε, χειμῶνος μὲν εὐχόμενοι θέρος,
θέρους δὲ χειμῶνα, καὶ καύματος μὲν ῥῖγος,
ῥίγους δὲ καῦμα καθάπερ οἱ νοσοῦντες δυσάρε-

yours is like a catamite's.[8] Indeed, no one
could tell the difference between you, given
the color of your cloaks, the softness and
abundance of your tunics, the scarves, the
shoes, the hairstyle, the perfume. You, "the
happiest ones," *reek* of perfume these days!
What would one give for a man who smells
exactly like a catamite? So it follows that you
tolerate hardship no more than they do, and
pleasures no less. You eat, sleep, and walk like
them, or rather, refuse to walk but are carried
around like cargo, some of you by human
beings, others by oxen. But me, my feet take
me wherever I need to go, and I am capable of
enduring heat and cold. I don't complain
about the gods' doings with "woe is me." You,
however, for all your happiness, are satisfied
with nothing that transpires, find fault with
everything, are unwilling to accept what you
have and yearn for what you don't, praying for
summer in winter and winter in summer, for
cold weather in hot and for hot weather in
cold. You're like hard-to-please invalids,
always complaining about your lot. Yet
disease is the cause of their complaining.
Yours is your way of life.

στοι καὶ μεμψίμοιροι ὄντες· αἰτία δὲ ἐκείνοις
μὲν ἡ νόσος, ὑμῖν δὲ ὁ τρόπος.

κἄπειτα δὲ ἡμᾶς μετατίθεσθε καὶ ἐπανορ-
θοῦτε τὰ ἡμέτερα, κακῶς βουλευομένοις
πολλάκις περὶ ὧν πράττομεν, αὐτοὶ ἄσκεπτοι
ὄντες περὶ τῶν ἰδίων καὶ μηδὲν αὐτῶν κρίσει
καὶ λογισμῷ ποιοῦντες, ἀλλ᾽ ἔθει καὶ ἐπιθυμίᾳ.
τοιγαροῦν οὐδὲν ὑμεῖς διαφέρετε τῶν ὑπὸ
χειμάρρου φερομένων· ἐκεῖνοί τε γάρ, ὅπου ἂν
ᾖ τὸ ῥεῦμα, ἐκεῖ φέρονται, καὶ ὑμεῖς ὅπου ἂν αἱ
ἐπιθυμίαι. πάσχετε δὲ παραπλήσιόν τι ὅ φασι
παθεῖν τινα ἐφ᾽ ἵππον ἀναβάντα μαινόμενον·
ἁρπάσας γὰρ αὐτὸν ἔφερεν ἄρα ὁ ἵππος· ὁ δὲ
οὐκέτι καταβῆναι τοῦ ἵππου θέοντος ἐδύνατο.
καί τις ἀπαντήσας ἠρώτησεν αὐτὸν ποίαν
ἄπεισιν; ὁ δὲ εἶπεν, Ὅπου ἂν τούτῳ δοκῇ,
δεικνὺς τὸν ἵππον. καὶ ὑμᾶς ἄν τις ἐρωτᾷ, ποῖ
φέρεσθε; τἀληθὲς ἐθέλοντες λέγειν ἐρεῖτε
ἁπλῶς μέν, ὅπουπερ ἂν ταῖς ἐπιθυμίαις δοκῇ,
κατὰ μέρος δέ, ὅπουπερ ἂν τῇ ἡδονῇ δοκῇ,
ποτὲ δέ, ὅπου τῇ δόξῃ, ποτὲ δὲ αὖ, τῇ φιλοκερ-
δίᾳ· ποτὲ δὲ ὁ θυμός, ποτὲ δὲ ὁ φόβος, ποτὲ δὲ
ἄλλο τι τοιοῦτον ὑμᾶς ἐκφέρειν φαίνεται· οὐ

And still you would change us and straighten out our affairs on the grounds that we often make poor choices in what we do, while you take *no* consideration for your own affairs and, when you do something, it is not based on decision-making or logic but on habit and appetite? You are no different from people who are carried away by a torrent: They are swept away in whatever direction the current takes them. You wherever your appetites take you. Your predicament is similar to what people say happens to someone mounted on a horse gone berserk: The horse bolts and carries the rider with it, and he is no longer able to dismount a horse at full gallop. Someone meets up with him and asks where he's heading to and he replies, pointing to the horse, "Wherever this one decides." So, if anyone should ask where you're heading, if you're willing to tell the truth, you'll say "Wherever my appetites decide," or, by turns, "my pleasure," or depending on the situation, "my greed, my temper, my fear" or whatever other emotion of this sort has swept you away. For you

γὰρ ἐφ᾽ ἑνός, ἀλλ᾽ ἐπὶ πολλῶν ὑμεῖς γε ἵππων
βεβηκότες ἄλλοτε ἄλλων, καὶ μαινομένων
πάντων, φέρεσθε. τοιγαροῦν ἐκφέρουσιν ὑμᾶς
εἰς βάραθρα καὶ κρημνούς. ἴστε δ᾽ οὐδαμῶς
πρὶν πεσεῖν ὅτι πείσεσθαι μέλλετε.

ὁ δὲ τρίβων οὗτος, οὗ καταγελᾶτε, καὶ ἡ
κόμη καὶ τὸ σχῆμα τοὐμὸν τηλικαύτην ἔχει
δύναμιν, ὥστε παρέχειν μοι ζῆν ἐφ᾽ ἡσυχίας καὶ
πράττοντι ὅ τι βούλομαι καὶ συνόντι οἷς
βούλομαι· τῶν γὰρ ἀμαθῶν ἀνθρώπων καὶ
ἀπαιδεύτων οὐδεὶς ἂν ἐθέλοι μοι προσιέναι διὰ
τὸ σχῆμα, οἱ δὲ μαλακοὶ καὶ πάνυ πόρρωθεν
ἐκτρέπονται· προσίασι δὲ οἱ κομψότατοι καὶ
ἐπιεικέστατοι καὶ ἀρετῆς ἐπιθυμοῦντες. οὗτοι
μάλιστά μοι προσίασι· τοῖς γὰρ τοιούτοις ἐγὼ
χαίρω συνών. θύρας δὲ τῶν καλουμένων
εὐδαιμόνων οὐ θεραπεύω, τοὺς δὲ χρυσοῦς
στεφάνους καὶ τὴν πορφύραν τῦφον νομίζω
καὶ τῶν ἀνθρώπων καταγελῶ.

ἵνα δὲ μάθῃς περὶ τοῦ σχήματος, ὡς οὐκ
ἀνδράσι μόνον ἀγαθοῖς, ἀλλὰ καὶ θεοῖς πρέπο-
ντος ἔπειτα καταγελᾷς αὐτοῦ, σκέψαι τὰ
ἀγάλματα τῶν θεῶν, πότερά σοι δοκοῦσιν
ὁμοίως ἔχειν ὑμῖν ἢ ἐμοί; καὶ μὴ μόνον γε τῶν

have not mounted one horse only, but many—different ones depending on the occasion—but all of them berserkers. In consequence, they are sweeping you off cliffs and into ravines, and you have no idea what's about to happen to you until you fall.

This old cloak, which you ridicule, and my hair and my whole getup gives me considerable power in that they allow me to live in peace and quiet, doing whatever I want with whomever I want. No ignorant or uneducated person would want to visit me given the way I dress, and the dandies turn away even from a long way's off. Those who do visit, however, are the most clever and decent people, desirous of virtue. These sorts come to visit me often and I happily spend time with them. But at the doors of the so-called happy people I pay no court. Rather I consider their golden crowns and purple robes nonsense and laugh at people who wear them.

And just so you know my costume suits not only good men, but also the gods, though you mock it, have a look at statues of gods. Do

Ἑλλήνων, ἀλλὰ καὶ τῶν βαρβάρων τοὺς ναοὺς
ἐπισκόπει περιιών, πότερον αὐτοὶ οἱ θεοὶ
κομῶσι καὶ γενειῶσιν ὡς ἐγὼ ἢ καθάπερ ὑμεῖς
ἐξυρημένοι πλάττονται καὶ γράφονται. καὶ
μέντοι καὶ ἀχίτωνας ὄψει τοὺς πολλοὺς ὥσπερ
ἐμέ. τί ἂν οὖν ἔτι τολμῴης περὶ τούτου τοῦ
σχήματος λέγειν ὡς φαῦλον, ὁπότε καὶ θεοῖς
φαίνεται πρέπον;

they look like you or do they look like me?
And not only the Greek gods. Go around and
inspect non-Greek temples, too, to see whether
the gods themselves have long hair and beards
like me, or whether they are sculpted and
painted, like you, clean-shaven. How then can
you still dare to say my style of dress is lousy
when it clearly is just fine even for gods?

9. Know Thyself!
(Julian, Oration 6, "To the Uneducated
Cynics," abridged)

*Julian was emperor of Rome from 361 to 363 CE.
He is sometimes called "the Apostate" because he
was raised a Christian but reverted as an adult to
the old beliefs of Hellenism. Indeed, he became
something of an evangelist for all things pagan. Julian was not a Cynic himself, favoring instead a
mystical form of Platonism. But he defends authentic Cynic practice here against an unnamed Cynic
interloper with considerable conviction. Julian's
learned eclecticism gives us a valuable perspective
on Cynicism's place in the larger context of Greek
philosophy. His appreciation of Diogenes as an oral-
ist and practitioner, for example, and his insistence
that philosophical pursuits are a divine mandate requiring deep, self-reflective critique, represent an
innovative interpretation of the evidence.*

Δεῦρο οὖν ἡμεῖς ὑπὲρ τῶν Κυνικῶν ὁπόσα διδα-
σκάλων ἠκούσαμεν ἐν κοινῷ καταθῶμεν σκοπεῖν
τοῖς ἐπὶ τὸν βίον ἰοῦσι τοῦτον· ...

Εἰ μὲν οὖν ἐπεποίητο τοῖς ἀνδράσι μετά τινος
σπουδῆς, ἀλλὰ μὴ μετὰ παιδιᾶς τὰ συγγράμματα,
τούτοις ἐχρῆν ἑπόμενον ἐπιχειρεῖν ἕκαστα ὧν διανοούμεθα περὶ τοῦ πράγματος ἐξετάζειν τὸν ἐνα-
ντίον καί, εἰ μὲν ἐφαίνετο τοῖς παλαιοῖς ὁμολο-
γοῦντα, μήτοι ψευδομαρτυριῶν ἡμῖν ἐπισκήπτειν,
εἰ δὲ μή, τότε ἐξορίζειν αὐτὰ τῆς ἀκοῆς ὥσπερ Ἀθηναῖοι τὰ ψευδῆ γράμματα τοῦ Μητρῴου. ἐπεὶ δὲ
οὐδέν ἐστιν, ὡς ἔφην, τοιοῦτον· αἵ τε γὰρ θρυλού-
μεναι Διογένους τραγῳδίαι Φιλίσκου τινὸς Αἰγι-
νήτου λέγονται εἶναι, καί, εἰ Διογένους δὴ εἶεν,
οὐδὲν ἄτοπόν ἐστι τὸν σοφὸν παίζειν, ἐπεὶ καὶ τοῦτο
πολλοὶ φαίνονται τῶν φιλοσόφων ποιήσαντες·
ἐγέλα τοι, φασί, καὶ Δημόκριτος ὁρῶν σπουδάζο-
ντας τοὺς ἀνθρώπους· ...

χρήσομαι γὰρ ἐκείνοις ἐγὼ τοῖς ῥήμασιν, οἷς
Ἀλκιβιάδης ἐπαινῶν Σωκράτη. φημὶ γὰρ δὴ τὴν
Κυνικὴν φιλοσοφίαν ὁμοιοτάτην εἶναι τοῖς Σειλη-
νοῖς τούτοις τοῖς ἐν τοῖς ἑρμογλυφείοις καθημέ-
νοις, οὕστινας ἐργάζονται οἱ δημιουργοὶ σύριγγας
ἢ αὐλοὺς ἔχοντας· οἳ διχάδε διοιχθέντες ἔνδον φαίνονται ἀγάλματα ἔχοντες θεῶν. ...

Now then, allow me to set forth publicly all that I have heard from my teachers about the Cynics so that those embarking upon this lifestyle can give it some thought. . . .

If the Cynics had composed written works with a measure of serious intent and not just for sport, a detractor would have to consult those works in any attempt to scrutinize my opinions on the subject. Then, if my views seemed to align with the ancient teachings, he ought not to bear false witness and denounce me. But if they don't align, then he should exclude my views from consideration, just as the Athenians expunge forged documents from the Metroön.[1] But no such situation exists, as I was saying earlier. For the storied tragedies of Diogenes are now said to be the work of one Philiscus from Aegina.[2] But even if they were in fact by Diogenes, there's nothing strange about a sage joking around. Many philosophers have done this. Indeed, they say Democritus in particular used to burst out laughing when he saw people taking themselves seriously.[3] . . .

To that point I will quote those well-known words Plato has Alcibiades use to praise Socrates.[4] For I assert that Cynic philosophy is just like those Silenus statuettes sitting in the statuary shops, which the craftsmen make holding Pan pipes or

λέγουσι μὲν γὰρ οἱ γενναιότεροι τῶν κυνῶν, ὅτι καὶ ὁ μέγας Ἡρακλῆς, ὥσπερ οὖν τῶν ἄλλων ἀγαθῶν ἡμῖν αἴτιος κατέστη, οὕτω δὲ καὶ τούτου τοῦ βίου παράδειγμα τὸ μέγιστον κατέλιπεν ἀνθρώποις. ἐγὼ δὲ ὑπὲρ τῶν θεῶν καὶ τῶν εἰς θείαν λῆξιν πορευθέντων εὐφημεῖν ἐθέλων πείθομαι μὲν καὶ πρὸ τούτου τινὰς οὐκ ἐν Ἕλλησι μόνον, ἀλλὰ καὶ βαρβάροις οὕτω φιλοσοφῆσαι· αὕτη γὰρ ἡ φιλοσοφία κοινή πως ἔοικεν εἶναι καὶ φυσικωτάτη καὶ δεῖσθαι οὐδ᾽ ἡστινοσοῦν πραγματείας· ἀλλὰ ἀπόχρη μόνον ἑλέσθαι τὰ σπουδαῖα ἀρετῆς ἐπιθυμίᾳ καὶ φυγῇ κακίας, καὶ οὔτε βίβλους ἀνελίξαι δεῖ μυρίας· πολυμαθία γάρ, φασί, νόον οὐ διδάσκει· οὔτε ἄλλο τι τῶν τοιούτων παθεῖν, ὅσα καὶ οἷα πάσχουσιν οἱ διὰ τῶν ἄλλων αἱρέσεων ἰόντες, ἀλλὰ ἀπόχρη μόνον δύο ταῦτα τοῦ Πυθίου παραινοῦντος ἀκοῦσαι, τὸ Γνῶθι σαυτὸν καὶ Παραχάραξον τὸ νόμισμα· πέφηνεν οὖν ἡμῖν ἀρχηγὸς τῆς φιλοσοφίας ὅσπερ οἶμαι τοῖς Ἕλλησι κατέστη τῶν καλῶν ἁπάντων αἴτιος, ὁ τῆς Ἑλλάδος κοινὸς ἡγεμὼν καὶ νομοθέτης καὶ βασιλεύς, ὁ ἐν Δελφοῖς θεός, ὃν ἐπειδὴ

shawms:[5] When you open them, pulling the halves apart, they have images of gods inside. . . .

Now the more authentic Cynics say the great Heracles is responsible for leaving behind for us a model for the Cynic way of life—just as responsible for that as he is for his other benefactions to humankind. While, for myself, I am keen to speak propitiously about the gods and those who have attained divine status, I nevertheless am convinced that even before Heracles there were people who followed this philosophy, not only among the Greeks, but among the non-Greeks too.[6] For Cynic philosophy seems somehow to be universal and most natural, needing no specialized study whatsoever. Simply to choose deliberate living from love of virtue and through avoidance of vice is enough. One need not leaf through countless books. For "much learning," as the saying goes, "does not teach intelligence."[7] Nor does one need to gain experience of the other matters that members of other philosophical sects do when they join up. Rather, it is enough to hearken to just these two injunctions from the Pythian god:[8] "Know thyself"; and "Deface the currency." It is clear to me from this that the founder of Cynic philosophy is in fact the god at Delphi, who is responsible, too, in my opinion, for all the good things the Greeks enjoy. He

μὴ θέμις ἦν τι διαλαθεῖν, οὐδὲ ἡ Διογένους ἐπιτη-
δειότης ἔλαθε. προύτρεψε δὲ αὐτὸν οὐχ ὥσπερ τοὺς
ἄλλους ἔπεσιν ἐντείνων τὴν παραίνεσιν, ἀλλ᾽ ἔργῳ
διδάσκων ὅ,τι βούλεται συμβολικῶς διὰ δυοῖν ὀνο-
μάτοιν, Παραχάραξον εἰπὼν τὸ νόμισμα· τὸ γάρ
Γνῶθι σαυτὸν οὐκ ἐκείνῳ μόνον, ἀλλὰ καὶ τοῖς ἄλλοις ἔφη καὶ λέγει, πρόκειται γὰρ οἶμαι τοῦ
τεμένους.

ηὑρήκαμεν δὴ τὸν ἀρχηγέτην τῆς φιλοσοφίας,
ὥς που καὶ ὁ δαιμόνιός φησιν Ἰάμβλιχος, ἀλλὰ καὶ
τοὺς κορυφαίους ἐν αὐτῇ, Ἀντισθένη καὶ Διογένη
καὶ Κράτητα, οἷς τοῦ βίου σκοπὸς ἦν καὶ τέλος
αὐτοὺς οἶμαι γνῶναι καὶ τῶν κενῶν ὑπεριδεῖν
δοξῶν, ἀληθείας δέ, ἣ πάντων μὲν ἀγαθῶν θεοῖς,
πάντων δὲ ἀνθρώποις ἡγεῖται, ὅλη, φασίν, ἐπι-
δράξασθαι τῇ διανοίᾳ, ἧς οἶμαι καὶ Πλάτων καὶ Πυθαγόρας καὶ Σωκράτης οἵ τε ἐκ τοῦ Περιπάτου καὶ
Ζήνων ἕνεκα πάντα ὑπέμειναν πόνον, αὑτούς τε
ἐθέλοντες γνῶναι καὶ μὴ κεναῖς ἕπεσθαι δόξαις,
ἀλλὰ τὴν ἐν τοῖς οὖσιν ἀλήθειαν ἀνιχνεῦσαι.

is Greece's joint leader, lawgiver, and king, and, since it would not be proper for anything to escape his notice, the suitability of Diogenes for his mission certainly did not escape it either. Apollo converted Diogenes to philosophy not by extending verbal advice, as he does for other people. Rather he taught him to do his will in action, symbolically, by means of two words: "deface" and "the currency."[9] "Know thyself," of course, he has uttered not only to Diogenes but to others as well—and utters it still since it is inscribed on his sanctuary.

And so we have discovered the founder of this philosophy, as the divine Iamblichus affirms somewhere as well.[10] We have discovered its chief proponents, too—Antisthenes, Diogenes, Crates—whose aim and goal in life was to know themselves, to disregard empty opinions, and apprehend the truth with their whole understanding. For truth is the source of all good things, for gods and human beings alike.[11] In my opinion, Plato, Pythagoras, Socrates, the Peripatetics,[12] and Zeno[13] all endured every hardship for its sake. They wished to know themselves and not to follow empty opinions but to track down the truth about what exists. . . .

Now then, since it's clear that Plato was not concerned with one thing and Diogenes with another

Φέρε οὖν, ἐπειδὴ πέφηνεν οὐκ ἄλλο μὲν ἐπιτη-
δεύσας Πλάτων, ἕτερον δὲ Διογένης, ἕν δέ τι καὶ
ταὐτόν· εἰ γοῦν ἔροιτό τις τὸν σοφὸν Πλάτωνα "τὸ
Γνῶθι σαυτὸν πόσου νενόμικας ἄξιον;" εὖ οἶδα ὅτι
τοῦ παντὸς ἂν φήσειε, καὶ λέγει δὲ ἐν Ἀλκιβιάδῃ·
δεῦρο δὴ τὸ μετὰ τοῦτο φράσον ἡμῖν, ὦ δαιμόνιε
Πλάτων καὶ θεῶν ἔκγονε "Τίνα τρόπον χρὴ πρὸς
τὰς τῶν πολλῶν διακεῖσθαι δόξας," ταῦτά τε ἐρεῖ
καὶ ἔτι πρὸς τούτοις ὅλον ἡμῖν ἐπιτάξει διαρρήδην
ἀναγνῶναι τὸν Κρίτωνα διάλογον, οὗ φαίνεται
παραινῶν Σωκράτης μηδὲν φροντίζειν ἡμᾶς τῶν
τοιούτων· φησὶ γοῦν· "Ἀλλὰ τί ἡμῖν, ὦ μακάριε
Κρίτων, οὕτω τῆς τῶν πολλῶν δόξης μέλει;" εἶτα
ἡμεῖς τούτων ὑπεριδόντες ἀποτειχίζειν ἁπλῶς
οὑτωσὶ καὶ ἀποσπᾶν ἄνδρας ἀλλήλων ἐθέλομεν,
οὓς ὁ τῆς ἀληθείας συνήγαγεν ἔρως ἥ τε τῆς δόξης
ὑπεροψία καὶ ἡ πρὸς τὸν ζῆλον τῆς ἀρετῆς ξύμπνοια;
εἰ δὲ Πλάτωνι μὲν ἔδοξε καὶ διὰ τῶν λόγων αὐτὰ
ἐργάζεσθαι, Διογένει δὲ ἀπέχρη τὰ ἔργα, διὰ τοῦτο
ἄξιός ἐστιν ὑφ᾽ ὑμῶν ἀκούειν κακῶς; ὅρα δὲ μὴ καὶ
τοῦτο αὐτὸ τῷ παντὶ κρεῖττόν ἐστιν, ἐπεὶ καὶ

but that their purpose was one and the same, if someone were to ask the wise Plato "What do you think the phrase 'know thyself' is worth?" I am certain he would say it's worth everything. Indeed, he says just this in the *Alcibiades*.[14] So come now, divine Plato, offspring of the gods, answer this second question: "What should be one's attitude toward the opinions of the multitude?" And he will say the same thing[15] and explicitly prescribe that we read his dialogue the *Crito*, where Socrates appears urging us not to pay attention to such opinions.[16] Actually, what he says is this: "But what concern is the opinion of the multitude to us, my blessed Crito?" So then, are we to disregard these similarities without thought and be so ready to wall off and pry apart men one from another whom the love of truth, disregard of opinion, and fellowship in zeal for virtue have joined together? If Plato thought it good to work out problems using words, whereas for Diogenes deeds sufficed, does Diogenes deserve the poor hearing he's getting from you because of that? Instead, consider whether that very thing—deeds— is not altogether superior, since even Plato swore off written works. As he says, "There is not, nor ever will be, any piece of writing by Plato. What's circulating these days belongs to Socrates—a man who's

Πλάτων ἐξομνύμενος φαίνεται τὰ ξυγγράμματα. "Οὐ γάρ ἐστι Πλάτωνος," φησί, "ζύγγραμμα οὐδὲν οὐδ᾽ ἔσται, τὰ δὲ νῦν φερόμενά ἐστι Σωκράτους, ἀνδρὸς καλοῦ καὶ νέου." τί οὖν ἡμεῖς οὐκ ἐκ τῶν ἔργων τοῦ Διογένους σκοποῦμεν αὐτὸν τὸν Κυνισμόν, ὅστις ἐστιν; . . .

ἐπεὶ καὶ Σωκράτης καὶ πλείονες ἄλλοι θεωρίᾳ μὲν φαίνονται χρησάμενοι πολλῇ, ταύτῃ δὲ οὐκ ἄλλου χάριν, ἀλλὰ τῆς πράξεως· ἐπεὶ καὶ τὸ ἑαυτὸν γνῶναι τοῦτο ἐνόμισαν, τὸ μαθεῖν ἀκριβῶς, τί μὲν ἀποδοτέον ψυχῇ, τί δὲ σώματι· ἀπέδοσαν δὲ εἰκότως ἡγεμονίαν μὲν τῇ ψυχῇ, ὑπηρεσίαν δὲ τῷ σώματι. φαίνονται δὴ οὖν ἀρετὴν ἐπιτηδεύσαντες, ἐγκράτειαν, ἀτυφίαν, ἐλευθερίαν, ἔξω γενόμενοι παντὸς φθόνου, δειλίας, δεισιδαιμονίας. ἀλλ᾽ οὐχ ἡμεῖς ταῦτα ὑπὲρ αὐτῶν διανοούμεθα, παίζειν δὲ αὐτοὺς καὶ κυβεύειν περὶ τοῖς φιλτάτοις ὑπολαμβάνομεν, οὕτως ὑπεριδόντας τοῦ σώματος, ὡς ὁ Σωκράτης ἔφη λέγων ὀρθῶς μελέτην εἶναι θανάτου τὴν φιλοσοφίαν. τοῦτο ἐκεῖνοι καθ᾽ ἑκάστην ἡμέραν ἐπιτηδεύοντες οὐ ζηλωτοὶ μᾶλλον ἡμῖν, ἄθλιοι δέ τινες καὶ παντελῶς ἀνόητοι δοκοῦσιν· ἀνθ᾽ ὅτου δὲ τοὺς

become beautiful and young again."[17] Why then should we not base our investigation of what Cynicism is on Diogenes's actions? . . .

Of course, Socrates and many others plainly engaged in plenty of theorizing. But it was theorizing for the sake of practice. For they reckoned that self-knowledge consists in discerning precisely what is the mind's responsibility and what is the body's. Quite reasonably, they assigned rulership to the mind and subservience to the body. And so, as is plain to see, these thinkers concerned themselves with virtue, self-control, sobriety, and freedom, and kept themselves well away from every kind of envy, cowardice, and superstition. But that's not what we've come to understand of them. Rather we suppose that, in disregarding the body, they were joking around and playing games about that most precious possession,[18] as when Socrates said—correctly—that philosophy is a rehearsal for death.[19] And although the Cynics made this their business every day (so the argument goes), we need not especially emulate them; in fact, certain ones among them seem wholly awful and stupid. But why did they endure those hardships? Not for the sake of vanity, as you have said. For how would they win praise from others by ingesting raw flesh? That, at any rate, has not won

πόνους ὑπέμειναν τούτους; οὐχ ὡς αὐτὸς εἶπας, κενοδοξίας ἕνεκα. καὶ γὰρ πῶς ὑπὸ τῶν ἄλλων ἐπηνοῦντο ὠμὰ προσφερόμενοι σαρκία; καίτοι οὐδὲ αὐτὸς ἐπαινέτης εἶ. τοῦ γοῦν τοιούτου τρίβωνα καὶ τὴν κόμην, ὥσπερ αἱ γραφαὶ τῶν ἀνδρῶν, ἀπομιμούμενος εἶθ᾽ ὃ μηδὲ αὐτὸς ἀξιάγαστον ὑπολαμβάνεις, τοῦτο εὐδοκιμεῖν οἴει παρὰ τῷ πλήθει; καὶ εἷς μὲν ἢ δεύτερος ἐπῄνει τότε, πλεῖν δ᾽ οὖν ἢ δέκα μυριάδες ὑπὸ τῆς ναυτίας καὶ βδελυρίας διεστράφησαν τὸν στόμαχον καὶ ἀπόσιτοι γεγόνασιν, ἄχρις αὐτοὺς οἱ θεράποντες ἀνέλαβον ὀσμαῖς καὶ μύροις καὶ πέμμασιν. οὕτως ὁ κλεινὸς ἥρως ἔργῳ κατεπλήξατο γελοίῳ μὲν ἀνθρώποις τοιούτοις,

Οἷοι νῦν βροτοί εἰσιν.

οὐκ ἀγεννεῖ δέ, μὰ τοὺς θεούς, εἴ τις αὐτὸ κατὰ τὴν Διογένους ἐξηγήσαιτο σύνεσιν. ὅπερ γὰρ ὁ Σωκράτης ὑπὲρ αὐτοῦ φησιν, ὅτι τῷ θεῷ νομίζων λατρείαν ἐκτελεῖν ἐν τῷ τὸν δοθέντα χρησμὸν ὑπὲρ αὐτοῦ κατὰ πάντα σκοπῶν ἐξετάζειν τὸν ἐλεγκτικὸν ἠσπάσατο βίον, τοῦτο καὶ Διογένης οἶμαι συνειδὼς

them your approval. Be that as it may, when you imitate them by donning an old cloak and wearing your
hair long as Cynics are depicted as doing in paint-
ings, even though you yourself don't think it admi-
rable, do you suppose you'll get a good reputation
with the crowd for this? One or two persons used to
praise a Cynic back in the day but more than a hundred thousand got sick to their stomachs with nau-
sea and disgust and went off their food until servants
would revive them with perfumes, biscuits, and
myrrh. That's the extent to which our notable hero
shocked people "such as mortals are these days"[20]
with absurd behavior.

And yet—the gods be my witness—it was not
sordid behavior, if you consider it from Diogenes's
perspective.[21] For Diogenes, I think, acted exactly
as Socrates says he did with respect to the oracle
that he received:[22] Socrates embraced a lifestyle
of cross-examining people thinking he was ful-
filling his service to the god Apollo, testing and
seeking out the full extent of the oracle's meaning; Diogenes, too, understood his philosophy as a
Pythian mandate and thought it incumbent on him
to cross-examine everything in action and not to be
influenced by others' opinions, which may be true,
but may also be false. Consequently, not even if

ἑαυτῷ, πυθόχρηστον οὖσαν τὴν φιλοσοφίαν, ἔργοις ᾤετο δεῖν ἐξελέγχειν πάντα καὶ μὴ δόξαις ἄλλων, τυχὸν μὲν ἀληθέσι, τυχὸν δὲ ψευδέσι προσπεπονθέναι. οὔκουν οὐδὲ εἴ τι Πυθαγόρας ἔφη, οὐδὲ εἴ τις ἄλλος τῷ Πυθαγόρᾳ παραπλήσιος, ἀξιόπιστος ἐδόκει τῷ Διογένει. τὸν γὰρ θεόν, ἀνθρώπων δὲ οὐδένα τῆς φιλοσοφίας ἀρχηγὸν ἐπεποίητο. . . .

Τῆς Κυνικῆς δὲ φιλοσοφίας σκοπὸς μέν ἐστι καὶ τέλος, ὥσπερ δὴ καὶ πάσης φιλοσοφίας, τὸ εὐδαιμονεῖν, τὸ δὲ εὐδαιμονεῖν ἐν τῷ ζῆν κατὰ φύσιν, ἀλλὰ μὴ πρὸς τὰς τῶν πολλῶν δόξας. ἐπεὶ καὶ τοῖς φυτοῖς εὖ πράττειν συμβαίνει καὶ μέντοι καὶ ζῴοις πᾶσιν, ὅταν τοῦ κατὰ φύσιν ἕκαστον ἀνεμποδίστως τυγχάνῃ τέλους· ἀλλὰ καὶ ἐν τοῖς θεοῖς τοῦτό ἐστιν εὐδαιμονίας ὅρος, τὸ ἔχειν αὐτοὺς ὥσπερ πεφύκασι καὶ ἑαυτῶν εἶναι. οὐκοῦν καὶ τοῖς ἀνθρώποις οὐχ ἑτέρωθί που τὴν εὐδαιμονίαν ἀποκεκρυμμένην προσήκει πολυπραγμονεῖν· οὐδὲ ἀετὸς οὐδὲ πλάτανος οὐδὲ ἄλλο τι τῶν ὄντων ζῴων ἢ φυτῶν χρυσᾶ περιεργάζεται πτερὰ καὶ φύλλα, οὐδὲ ὅπως

Pythagoras uttered a pronouncement, or someone with the gravitas of a Pythagoras, would Diogenes think it necessarily true. For it was his conviction that the god at Delphi, not a human being, was the founder of his philosophy. . . .

The end and outlook of Cynic philosophy, as in fact of all philosophy, is to be happy. But Cynics seek a happiness that arises from living according to Nature, with no deference to the opinions of the multitude. Plants also flourish, as indeed do all the animals, when each one achieves its natural end with no impediments. In fact, this is the definition of happiness among the gods, too, namely that they live in their natural state and with autonomy. Likewise for human beings—we shouldn't run around looking for happiness as if it lay hidden outside of ourselves. Neither an eagle, nor a plane tree, nor any other animal or plant concerns itself about having wings or leaves made of gold, or new growth of silver, or spurs and thorns of iron or adamantine. No, they would think they're positively thriving and have been well provided for with what Nature adorned them with at the start, so long as their natural endowments ensure strength for speed or are serviceable for protection. How then is it not ridiculous for a person to seek happiness

ἀργυροῦς ἕξει τοὺς βλαστοὺς ἢ τὰ πλῆκτρα καὶ κέ-
ντρα σιδηρᾶ, μᾶλλον δὲ ἀδαμάντινα, ἀλλ᾽ οἷς αὐτὰ
ἐξ ἀρχῆς ἡ φύσις ἐκόσμησε, ταῦτα εἰ ῥωμαλέα καὶ
πρὸς τάχος αὐτοῖς ἢ πρὸς ἀλκὴν ὑπουργοῦντα
προσγένοιτο, μάλιστα ἂν εὖ πράττειν νομίζοι καὶ
εὐθηνεῖσθαι. πῶς οὖν οὐ γελοῖον, εἴ τις ἄνθρωπος
γεγονὼς ἔξω που τὴν εὐδαιμονίαν περιεργάσαιτο,
πλοῦτον καὶ γένος καὶ φίλων δύναμιν καὶ πάντα
ἁπλῶς τὰ τοιαῦτα τοῦ παντὸς ἄξια νομίζων; εἰ μὲν
οὖν ἡμῖν ἡ φύσις ὥσπερ τοῖς ζῴοις αὐτὸ τοῦτο ἀπέ-
δωκε μόνον, τὸ σώματα καὶ ψυχὰς ἔχειν ἐκείνοις
παραπλησίας, ὥστε μηδὲν πλέον πολυπραγμονεῖν, ἤρκει λοιπόν, ὥσπερ τὰ λοιπὰ ζῷα, τοῖς σω-
ματικοῖς ἀρκεῖσθαι πλεονεκτήμασιν, ἐνταῦθά που
τὸ εὐδαιμονεῖν πολυπραγμονοῦσιν. ἐπεὶ δὲ ἡμῖν
οὐδέν τι παραπλησία ψυχὴ τοῖς ἄλλοις ἐνέσπαρ-
ται ζῴοις, ἀλλ᾽ εἴτε κατ᾽ οὐσίαν διαφέρουσα εἴτε
οὐσίᾳ μὲν ἀδιάφορος, ἐνεργείᾳ δὲ μόνῃ κρείττων,
ὥσπερ οἶμαι τὸ καθαρὸν ἤδη χρυσίον τοῦ συμπε-
φυρμένου τῇ ψάμμῳ· λέγεται γὰρ καὶ οὗτος ὁ
λόγος περὶ τῆς ψυχῆς ὡς ἀληθὴς ὑπό τινων· ἡμεῖς
δὴ οὖν ἐπειδὴ σύνισμεν αὐτοῖς οὖσι τῶν ζῴων ξυνε-
τωτέροις· κατὰ γὰρ τὸν Πρωταγόρου μῦθον ἐκείνοις μὲν ἡ φύσις ὥσπερ μήτηρ ἄγαν φιλοτίμως καὶ
μεγαλοδώρως προσηνέχθη, ἡμῖν δὲ ἀντὶ πάντων
ἐκ Διὸς ὁ νοῦς ἐδόθη· τὴν εὐδαιμονίαν ἐνταῦθα

somewhere outside himself and to count wealth, birth, influential friends and basically all things of that sort as worth everything in the world? If Nature gave us only what it gave other living creatures—that is, to have bodies and souls like theirs so that we need not concern ourselves with anything else—then it would suit us, as it suits the other animals, to find fulfillment in physical advantages and pursue happiness in that domain. But the soul implanted in us is nothing like the souls of other animals. Who knows whether it is fundamentally different or just superior in its activity, analogous perhaps to how pure gold is superior to gold alloyed with sand (an account of the soul that is held to be true by some scholars). Regardless, we are certainly cognizant of being more intelligent than the other animals. According to the myth told by Protagoras,[23] Nature treated the animals lavishly and with considerable munificence at their creation. To us, however, by way of compensation for all that, Mind was given by Zeus. Happiness, then, must reside there, in that most powerful and important part of us.

Consider then whether or not Diogenes was very much a man of this conviction: He would

θετέον, ἐν τῷ κρατίστῳ καὶ σπουδαιοτάτῳ τῶν ἐν ἡμῖν.

Σκόπει δή, ταύτης εἰ μὴ μάλιστα τῆς προαιρέσεως ἦν Διογένης, ὃς τὸ μὲν σῶμα τοῖς πόνοις ἀνέδην παρεῖχεν, ἵνα αὐτὸ τῆς φύσεως ῥωμαλεώτερον καταστήσῃ, πράττειν δὲ ἠξίου μόνον ὁπόσα ἂν φανῇ τῷ λόγῳ πρακτέα, τοὺς δὲ ἐκ τοῦ σώματος ἐμπίπτοντας τῇ ψυχῇ θορύβους, οἷα πολλάκις ἡμᾶς ἀναγκάζει τουτὶ τὸ περικείμενον αὐτοῦ χάριν πολυπραγμονεῖν, οὐδὲ ἐν μέρει προσίετο. ὑπὸ δὲ ταύτης τῆς ἀσκήσεως ὁ ἀνὴρ οὕτω μὲν ἔσχεν ἀνδρεῖον τὸ σῶμα ὡς οὐδεὶς οἶμαι τῶν τοὺς στεφανίτας ἀγωνισαμένων, οὕτω δὲ διετέθη τὴν ψυχήν, ὥστε εὐδαιμονεῖν, ὥστε βασιλεύειν οὐδὲν ἔλαττον, εἰ μὴ καὶ πλέον, ὡς οἱ τότε εἰώθεσαν λέγειν Ἕλληνες, τοῦ μεγάλου βασιλέως, τὸν Πέρσην λέγοντες. ἆρά σοι μικρὰ φαίνεται ἀνὴρ

Ἄπολις, ἄοικος, πατρίδος ἐστερημένος,
οὐκ ὀβολόν, οὐ δραχμήν, ἔχων οὐδ᾽ οἰκέτην,

ἀλλ᾽ οὐδὲ μᾶζαν, ἧς Ἐπίκουρος εὐπορῶν οὐδὲ τῶν θεῶν φησιν εἰς εὐδαιμονίας λόγον ἐλαττοῦσθαι, πρὸς μὲν τοὺς θεοὺς οὐκ ἐρίζων, τοῦ δοκοῦντος δὲ τοῖς ἀνθρώποις εὐδαιμονεστάτου εὐδαιμονέστερον ζῶν καὶ ἔλεγε ζῆν εὐδαιμονέστερον.

subject his body to hardships of his own free will in order to make it stronger than it naturally was; he was guided solely by reason in choosing how to behave; and to the troubles that arise from the body to beset the soul, such that this mortal frame often compels us to take many pains for its sake, he paid no heed at all. By means of this training the man possessed a body more manly, I believe, than any athlete competing for wreaths of victory. His psychic disposition, too, was such that he was happy and lived like a king no less—if not more— than the Great King himself (as Greeks back then used to call the Persian monarch). Does our man really seem small to you because he was "city-less, homeless, bereft of his country, having neither obol nor drachma nor slave"—or even his bread? (About bread Epicurus says that so long as he has enough of it, in a happiness reckoning, he's not inferior to the gods.) While Diogenes didn't vie with the gods, he did live more happily than anyone who thought himself the happiest human being. Diogenes actually used to say he lived more happily than such a person. And if you don't believe me, try out his lifestyle in action and not just with talk and you'll see for yourself. . . .

εἰ δὲ ἀπιστεῖς, ἔργῳ πειραθεὶς ἐκείνου τοῦ βίου καὶ
οὐ τῷ λόγῳ αἰσθήσῃ. . . .

Ἀλλ᾽ ἐπανίωμεν ἐπ᾽ ἐκεῖνο πάλιν, ὅτι χρὴ τὸν
ἀρχόμενον κυνίζειν αὐτῷ πρότερον ἐπιτιμᾶν πικρῶς
καὶ ἐξελέγχειν καὶ μὴ κολακεύειν, ἀλλὰ ἐξετάζειν ὅ,
τι μάλιστα αὐτὸν ἀκριβῶς, εἰ τῇ πολυτελείᾳ τῶν σιτίων χαίρει, εἰ στρωμνῆς δεῖται μαλακῆς, εἰ τιμῆς ἢ
δόξης ἐστὶν ἥττων, εἰ τοῦτο ζηλοῖ τὸ περιβλέπεσθαι
καί, εἰ καὶ κενὸν εἴη, τίμιον ὅμως νομίζει. μηδὲ εἰς
συμπεριφορὰν ὄχλων καθυφείσθω, γευέσθω δὲ
τρυφῆς μηδὲ ἄκρῳ, φασί, τῷ δακτύλῳ, ἕως ἂν
αὐτὴν παντελῶς πατήσῃ. τότε ἤδη καὶ τῶν τοιούτων,
ἂν προσπίπτῃ, θιγεῖν οὐδὲν κωλύει. ἐπεὶ καὶ τῶν
ταύρων ἀκούω τοὺς ἀσθενεστέρους ἐξίστασθαι τῆς
ἀγέλης καὶ καθ᾽ ἑαυτοὺς νεμομένους ἀγείρειν τὴν
ἰσχὺν ἐν μέρει καὶ κατ᾽ ὀλίγον, εἶθ᾽ οὕτως ἐπιέναι
καὶ προκαλεῖσθαι καὶ τῆς ἀγέλης ἀμφισβητεῖν τοῖς
προκατέχουσιν, ὡς μᾶλλον ἀξιωτέρους προΐστασθαι.
ὅστις οὖν κυνίζειν ἐθέλει μήτε τὸν τρίβωνα μήτε τὴν
πήραν μήτε τὴν βακτηρίαν καὶ τὴν κόμην ἀγαπάτω
μόνον, ἵν᾽ ὥσπερ ἐν κώμῃ βαδίζῃ κουρείων καὶ δι-
δασκαλείων ἐνδεεῖ ἄκαρτος καὶ ἀγράμματος, ἀλλὰ

KNOW THYSELF!

But let us return to my earlier point that anyone embarking on the Cynic life ought to censure himself severely, to cross-examine and not to engage in self-aggrandizement, but to ask himself the following questions in no uncertain terms: Do I enjoy expensive food? Must I have a soft bed? Do I pander to honor and reputation? Do I crave attention and, even though it be vacuous, count it as honorific nonetheless? Let anyone interested in Cynicism not give in to the complacency of the mob, nor sample luxury with even the tip of his finger, as they say, until he has trampled it entirely underfoot. Only when he has done that might he touch the finer things if they happen to present themselves. I hear it said, for example, that bulls who are rather weak stand apart from the herd and pasture by themselves in order to regain their strength gradually, bit by bit. Then they return to the group thus restored and summon the alpha bulls to vie with them for supremacy, thinking they are fitter now to be the front-runner. So, if you want to be a Cynic, don't just go in for the cloak, the knapsack, the walking stick, and long hair, as if you were walking about, unshorn and unlettered, in a village with no barber shops or schools. No, understand rather that ratio-

τὸν λόγον ἀντὶ τοῦ σκήπτρου καὶ τὴν ἔνστασιν ἀντὶ τῆς πήρας τῆς κυνικῆς ὑπολαμβανέτω φιλοσοφίας γνωρίσματα. . . .

Εἰ δὲ ἑταίρᾳ ποτὲ προσῆλθεν ὁ ἀνήρ· καίτοι καὶ τοῦτο τυχὸν ἅπαξ ἢ οὐδὲ ἅπαξ ἐγένετο· ὅταν ἡμῖν τὰ ἄλλα κατὰ τὸν Διογένη γένηται σπουδαῖος, ἂν αὐτῷ φανῇ καὶ τοιοῦτόν τι δρᾶν φανερῶς ἐν ὀφθαλμοῖς πάντων, οὐ μεμψόμεθα οὐδὲ αἰτιασόμεθα. πρότερον μέντοι τὴν Διογένους ἡμῖν ἐπιδειξάμενος εὐμάθειαν καὶ τὴν ἀγχίνοιαν καὶ τὴν ἐν τοῖς ἄλλοις ἅπασιν ἐλευθερίαν, αὐτάρκειαν, δικαιοσύνην, σωφροσύνην, εὐλάβειαν, χάριν, προσοχήν, ὡς μηδὲν εἰκῆ μηδὲ μάτην μηδὲ ἀλόγως ποιεῖν· ἐπεὶ καὶ ταῦτα τῆς Διογένους ἐστὶ φιλοσοφίας οἰκεῖα· πατείτω τῦφον, καταπαιζέτω τῶν τὰ μὲν ἀναγκαῖα τῆς φύσεως ἔργα κρυπτόντων ἐν σκότῳ· φημὶ δὲ τῶν περιττωμάτων τὰς ἐκκρίσεις· ἐν μέσαις δὲ ταῖς ἀγοραῖς καὶ ταῖς πόλεσιν ἐπιτηδευόντων τὰ βιαιότατα καὶ μηδὲν ἡμῶν οἰκεῖα τῇ φύσει, χρημάτων ἁρπαγάς, συκοφαντίας, γραφὰς ἀδίκους, διώξεις ἄλλων τοιούτων συρφετωδῶν πραγμάτων. ἐπεὶ καὶ Διογένης εἴτε ἀπέπαρδεν εἴτε ἀπεπάτησεν εἴτε ἄλλο τι τοιοῦτον ἔπραξεν, ὥσπερ οὖν λέγουσιν, ἐν

nality, not a staff, and way of life, not a knapsack, are the hallmarks of Cynic philosophy. . . .

And if Diogenes sometimes visited a prostitute, well, this happened but once, or not even once. Yet if someone serious about Diogenes in other respects were to decide to do the same, openly, before the eyes of all, for our part we will not blame him or find fault—if, that is, he has already displayed to us Diogenes's cleverness and quick wit, his freedom in all other matters, his self-sufficiency, righteousness, self-control, his awareness, gratitude, and careful concern not to do anything at random or to no effect or without good reason, since these are also part and parcel of Diogenes's philosophy. Let him trample on pretense. Let him make fun of people who hide under cover of darkness what are necessary, natural functions. What I mean is the secretion of what is superfluous.[24] And yet those same people busy themselves in the middle of our marketplaces and cities with the most outrageous behavior, inappropriate to our nature: stealing money, sycophantic conniving, unjust lawsuits, and the pursuit of other rubbish of this sort. Whereas, when Diogenes farted or shat or did anything else like that in the marketplace, as they say he did, his actions were aimed at trampling on the

ἀγορᾷ, τὸν ἐκείνων πατῶν τῦφον ἐποίει, διδάσκων αὐτούς, ὅτι πολλῷ φαυλότερα καὶ χαλεπώτερα τούτων ἐπιτηδεύουσι. τὰ μὲν γάρ ἐστιν ἡμῖν πᾶσι κατὰ φύσιν, τὰ δὲ ὡς ἔπος εἰπεῖν οὐδενί, πάντα δὲ ἐκ διαστροφῆς ἐπιτηδεύεται.

Ἀλλ᾽ οἱ νῦν τοῦ Διογένους ζηλωταὶ τὸ ῥᾷστον καὶ κουφότατον ἑλόμενοι τὸ κρεῖττον οὐκ εἶδον· σύ τε ἐκείνων εἶναι σεμνότερος ἐθέλων ἀπεπλανήθης τοσοῦτον τῆς Διογένους προαιρέσεως, ὥστε αὐτὸν ἐλεεινὸν ἐνόμισας. εἰ δὲ τούτοις μὲν ἠπίστεις ὑπὲρ ἀνδρὸς λεγομένοις, ὃν οἱ πάντες Ἕλληνες τότε ἐθαύμασαν μετὰ Σωκράτη καὶ Πυθαγόραν ἐπὶ Πλάτωνος καὶ Ἀριστοτέλους, οὗ γέγονεν ἀκροατὴς ὁ τοῦ σωφρονεστάτου καὶ συνετωτάτου Ζήνωνος καθηγεμών, οὓς οὐκ εἰκὸς ἦν ἅπαντας ἀπατηθῆναι περὶ ἀνδρὸς οὕτω φαύλου, ὁποῖον σὺ διακωμῳδεῖς, ὦ βέλτιστε, ἴσως ἄν τι πλέον ἐσκόπησας περὶ αὐτοῦ καὶ πορρωτέρω προῆλθες τῆς ἐμπειρίας τἀνδρός. τίνα γὰρ οὐκ ἐξέπληξε τῶν Ἑλλήνων ἡ Διογένους καρτερία, βασιλικῆς οὐκ ἔξω μεγαλοψυχίας οὖσα, καὶ φιλοπονία; ἐκάθευδεν ἀνὴρ ἐπὶ στιβάδος ἐν τῷ πίθῳ βέλτιον ἢ μέγας βασιλεὺς ὑπὸ τοῖς ἐπιχρύσοις ὀρόφοις ἐν τῇ μαλθακῇ κλίνῃ, ἤσθιε τὴν μᾶζαν

172

pretense of those people, to teach them that they were engaged in business much more sordid and problematic than his. For those activities are natural to us all, whereas their activities, to put it plainly, are natural to no one. To engage in all such things springs from a perversion of Nature.

But the Diogenes imitators of today have opted for the lightest and easiest path and have not noticed the better one. You yourself, wanting to be held in higher esteem than the Cynics of old, have strayed so far from Diogenes's way of life that you thought him to be pitied. And if you've disbelieved my account of a man whom, in the time of Plato and Aristotle, all the Greeks admired on par with Socrates and Pythagoras, whose disciple was the mentor of Zeno,[25] a highly intelligent and disciplined man, well then, Your Excellency, just perhaps you should have dug a little deeper in your research about Diogenes and you would have made better progress in obtaining evidence about him. It would be unlikely for the philosophers mentioned above to have been deceived about a man your caricature suggests was worthless. In fact, was there any Greek whom Diogenes's toughness and embrace of hardship did not astound, which had in it a royal magnanimity? The man slept in a storage jar

ἥδιον ἢ σὺ νῦν τὰς Σικελικὰς ἐσθίεις τραπέζας, ἐλούετο ψυχρῷ τὸ σῶμα πρὸς ἀέρα ξηραίνων ἀντὶ τῶν ὀθονίων, οἷς σὺ ἀπομάττῃ, φιλοσοφώτατε. πάνυ σοι προσήκει κωμῳδεῖν ἐκεῖνον, ὅτι κατειργάσω τὸν Ξέρξην, ὡς ὁ Θεμιστοκλῆς, ἢ τὸν Δαρεῖον, ὡς ὁ Μακεδὼν Ἀλέξανδρος. εἰ σμικρὰ τὰς βίβλους ἀνελίττων ἐμελέτας ὥσπερ ἡμεῖς οἱ πολιτικοὶ καὶ πολυπράγμονες, ἔγνως ἄν, ὅπως Ἀλέξανδρος ἀγασθῆναι λέγεται τὴν Διογένους μεγαλοψυχίαν. ἀλλ' οὐκ ἔστι σοι τούτων οὐδέν, ὡς ἐμοὶ δοκεῖ, σπουδαῖον·

Εἰ μὲν οὖν ὁ λόγος τι πλέον ἐποίησεν, οὐκ ἐμὸν μᾶλλον ἢ σόν ἐστι κέρδος· εἰ δὲ οὐδὲν περαίνομεν ἐκ τοῦ παραχρῆμα περὶ τῶν τοιούτων ἀπνευστὶ τὸ δὴ λεγόμενον συνείραντες· ἔστι γὰρ πάρεργον ἡμέραιν δυοῖν, ὡς ἴσασιν αἱ Μοῦσαι, μᾶλλον δὲ καὶ σὺ αὐτός· παραμενέτω μέν σοι ὁπόσα πρόσθεν ἐγνώκεις, ἡμῖν δὲ οὐ μεταμελήσει τῆς εἰς τὸν ἄνδρα εὐφημίας.

on a bed of straw more soundly than the Great King on his soft chaise longue under gilded ceilings! He ate his plain bread with more gusto than you eat your fine Sicilian cuisine! He would bathe in cold water and then dry off in open air—a far cry from the linen cloths you towel yourself off with, Thou Most Great Lover of Wisdom! It entirely befits you to make fun of Diogenes, since, like Themistocles, you repelled Xerxes, or, like Alexander, you defeated Darius.[26] If you had a smidgen of care to thumb through books as I do—me a government official and a busy man!—you would have known that Alexander is said to have admired Diogenes's big heartedness. But it seems to me you have no enthusiasm for books. . . .

And so, if my discourse has achieved anything, the advantage will be more yours than mine. But if I am accomplishing nothing in having strung together here a treatise on these matters off-the-cuff, without taking a breath, as they say, then by all means keep to your former opinions. As the Muses know full well—or rather as do you yourself—this work has been but a diversion of two days' time. And yet I will not repent the due respect I have extended to that man.

10. The Columnist

(Theodoret, *Life of Symeon Stylites*, abridged)

At least two Christian saints called Symeon display Cynic-like traits. The bona fides of Symeon the Holy Fool (522–588 CE) are perhaps the more apparent. This Symeon announced his debut in Emesa, Syria by dragging a dead dog through the streets. He defecated and farted copiously in public, ate raw meat, and cavorted with prostitutes—all somehow to the greater glory of God.[1] The reason for the strong Cynic resemblance is that his hagiographer, Leontius, a bishop from Cyprus, intentionally drew upon the Diogenes tradition in constructing his Life.[2] *In contrast to Leontius's self-conscious, literary treatment, the eyewitness account of Symeon Stylites (390–459 CE) by Theodoret, which is abridged here, showcases a more intriguing, sociohistorical parallel between Christian and Cynic asceticism that arguably goes all the way back to Jesus himself. ("Foxes have holes and birds of the air have nests, but the Son of Man hath not where to lay his head.") This earlier Symeon was nicknamed Stylites, or "the Columnist," because he made his home atop a fifty-foot pillar just outside of Aleppo. From here*

Συμεώνην τὸν πάνυ, τὸ μέγα θαῦμα τῆς οἰκουμένης, ἴσασι μὲν ἅπαντες οἱ τῆς Ῥωμαίων ἡγεμονίας ὑπήκοοι, ἔγνωσαν δὲ καὶ Πέρσαι καὶ Μῆδοι καὶ Αἰθίοπες, καὶ πρὸς Σκύθας δὲ τοὺς νομάδας ἡ φήμη δραμοῦσα τὴν τοῦδε φιλοπονίαν καὶ φιλοσοφίαν ἐδίδαξεν. Ἐγὼ δὲ καὶ πάντας, ὡς ἔπος εἰπεῖν, ἀνθρώπους μάτυρας ἔχων τῶν ὑπὲρ λόγον ἀγώνων δέδοικα τὸ διήγημα μὴ τοῖς ἐσσομένοις μῦθος εἶναι δόξῃ πάμπαν τῆς ἀληθείας γεγυμνωμένος. Ὑψηλότερα γὰρ τῆς ἀνθρωπείας φύσεως μετρεῖν τὰ λεγόμενα. Εἰ δέ τι τῶν ταύτης ὅρων ἐπέκεινα λέγοιτο, ψευδὴς τοῖς τῶν θείων ἀμυήτοις ὁ λόγος νομίζεται. Ἐπειδὴ δὲ τῶν εὐσεβούντων γῆ καὶ θάλαττα πλήρης, οἵ τε τὰ θεῖα πεπαιδευμένοι καὶ τοῦ παναγίου πνεύματος τὴν χάριν δεδιαγμένοι τοῖς λεχθησομένοις οὐκ ἀπιστήσουσιν, ἀλλὰ καὶ μάλα πιστεύσουσι, προθύμως καὶ θαρσαλέως ποιήσομαι

he practiced devotion, dispensed wisdom, and set-
tled disputes for thirty-seven years. Theodoret's
appeal to the performative acts of Old Testament
prophets as a comparand for Symeon's own un-
usual behavior is an inspired observation, suggesting
that every age and every tradition seems to create
the Dog in its own image, as D'Alembert once sug-
gested it must.[3]

All subjects of the Roman Empire know the excellent Symeon, that great wonder of the inhab-
ited world. Persians, Medes, and Ethiopians have
come to know of him, too, as his fame has spread
quickly, even to the nomadic Scythians, and has
taught them about his love of wisdom and endurance. And yet, even though I have all humanity, so
to speak, as my witness of his labors that defy
comprehension, I fear my account will seem to
posterity to be a myth, stripped entirely of the
truth. For the events of his life do rise above
human nature, and people tend to measure what is
said against Nature. Thus, if a statement exceeds
Nature's limits in any way, it is reckoned false by
those uninitiated into the divine mysteries. But
since earth and sea are filled with pious individuals educated in divine matters who have been

τὴν διήγησιν. Ἄρξομαι δὲ ἐκεῖθεν, ὅθεν καὶ τῆς ἄνωθεν κλήσεως ἠξιώθη.

Κώμη τίς ἐστιν ἐν μεθορίῳ τῆς ἡμετέρας καὶ τῆς Κιλίκων χώρας διακειμένην· Σισὰν δὲ αὐτὴν ὀνομάζουσιν. Ἐκ ταύτης ὁρμώμενος ποιμαίνειν τὸ πρῶτον ὑπὸ τῶν γεγεννηκότων ἐδιδάσκετο θρέμματα ἵνα καὶ κατὰ τοῦτο τοῖς μεγάλοις ἀνδράσι συμφέρηται, Ἰακὼβ τῷ πατριάρχῃ καὶ Ἰωσὴφ τῷ σώφρονι καὶ Μωυσῇ τῷ νομοθέτῃ καὶ Δαβὶδ τῷ βασιλεῖ καὶ προφήτῃ καὶ Μιχαίᾳ τῷ προφήτῃ καὶ τοῖς κατ' ἐκείνους θεσπεσίοις ἀνδράσι. Νιφετοῦ δέ ποτε πολλοῦ γενομένου καὶ τῶν προβάτων ἔνδον μένειν ἠναγκασμένων, ἀνακωχῆς ἀπολαύσας εἰς τὸν θεῖον νεὼν μετὰ τῶν φυσάντων ἀφίκετο. Ταῦτα δὲ τῆς ἱερᾶς αὐτοῦ διηγουμένης ἀκήκοα γλώττης. Ἔφη τοίνυν τῆς εὐαγγελικῆς ἀκηκοέναι φωνῆς μακαριζούσης μὲν τοὺς κλαίοντας καὶ πενθοῦντας, ἀθλίους δὲ τοὺς γελῶντας ἀποκαλούσης καὶ ζηλωτοὺς ὀνομαζούσης τοὺς τοὺς τὴν ψυχὴν καθαρὰν κεκτημένους καὶ τὰ ἄλλα ὅσα τούτοις συνέζευκται· εἶτα ἐρέσθαι τινὰ τῶν παρόντων τί ἄν τις ποιήσας τούτων ἕκαστον κτήσαιτο τὸν δὲ τὸν μοναδικὸν αὐτῷ βίον ὑπαγορεῦσαι καὶ τὴν ἄκραν ἐκείνην ὑποδεῖξαι φιλοσοφίαν.

taught by the grace of the All-Holy Spirit and will not doubt what I have to say, but believe it in earnest, I shall render my account eagerly and with confidence. I shall begin from that moment when Symeon was deemed fit to receive his calling from above.

There is a village situated on the border between our region[4] and Cilicia called Sisa. Symeon grew up there and was taught by his parents early on to pasture the flocks, so that even in this respect he was comparable to great men like the patriarch Jacob, prudent Joseph, Moses the lawgiver, the prophetic King David, the prophet Micah, and inspired men of that kind. One particularly snowy day, when the sheep were penned up inside, he took a break from shepherding and went to God's temple with his parents. I heard his holy tongue recount these details. He said he heard the voice of the Gospel bless those who weep and mourn, declare wretched those who laugh, and pronounce those who have acquired a pure soul enviable, and as many other beatitudes are linked to these.[5] He said he then asked someone in the congregation what someone must do to gain each of these blessings and he suggested to him the solitary life and so introduced him to that highest form of philosophy.

Δεξάμενος τοίνυν τοῦ θείου λόγου τὰ σπέρματα καὶ ταῖς βαθείαις τῆς ψυχῆς αὔλαξι ταῦτα καλῶς κατακρύψας εἰς τὸν πελάζοντα τῶν ἁγίων μαρτύρων ἔφη δεδραμηκέναι σηκόν. Ἐν τούτῳ δὲ τῇ γῇ τὰ γόνατα καὶ τὸ μέτωπον προσερεῖσαί τε καὶ ἱκετεῦσαι τὸν πάντας ἀνθρώπους σῴζειν ἐθέλοντα ποδηγῆσαι αὐτὸν πρὸς τὴν τελείαν τῆς εὐσεβείας ὁδόν. Ἐπὶ πολὺ δὲ τοῦτον διατρίψαντι τὸν τρόπον ὕπνον μὲν αὐτῷ προσγενέσθαι τινὰ γλυκύν, ὄναρ δὲ τοιόνδε θεάσασθαι· "Ὀρύττειν, φησίν, ἐδόκουν θεμέλια, εἶτά τινος ἑστῶτος ἀκούειν, ὡς ἔτι με βαθύνειν τὸ ὄρυγμα δεῖ. Προστεθεικὼς τοίνυν ὡς ἐκέλευσε βάθος πάλιν ἐπειρώμην διαναπαύεσθαι. Ἀλλὰ καὶ αὖθίς μοι ὀρύττειν προσέταττε καὶ μὴ λήγειν τοῦ πόνου. Τρὶς δέ μοι τοῦτο καὶ τετράκις ποιῆσαι παρεγγυήσας τέλος ἀποχρώντως ἔχειν ἔφη τὸ βάθος καὶ οἰκοδομεῖν ἀπόνως ἐκέλευσε τὸ λοιπὸν ὡς τοῦ πόνου λωφήσαντος καὶ τῆς οἰκοδομίας ἐσομένης ἀπόνως." Ταύτῃ τῇ προρρήσει τὰ πράγματα μαρτυρεῖ· πέρα γὰρ τῆς φύσεως τὰ γιγνόμενα.

Ἐκεῖθεν ἀναστὰς ἀσκητῶν τινων γειτονευόντων κατέλαβε καταγώγιον. Δύο δὲ αὐτοῖς συνδιαγαγὼν ἔτη καὶ τῆς τελειοτέρας ἀρετῆς ἐρασθεὶς Τελεδὰν ἐκείνην τὴν κώμην κατέλαβεν ... παρ' ἣν οἱ μεγάλοι καὶ θεῖοι ἄνδρες Ἀμμιανὸς καὶ Εὐσέβιος τὴν ἀσκητικὴν παλαίστραν ἐπήξαντο.... Ὀλίγον τοί-

He thus received the seeds of God's word and planted them well in the deep furrows of his soul. He says he then ran to the neighboring shrine of the Holy Martyrs where he bent face and knees to the ground and supplicated Him who wishes to save all people to direct his feet on the perfect path of piety. When he had lived in this manner for some time, a sweet sleep came over him and he saw the following dream: "I seemed to be digging foundations," he told me, "and heard someone standing by say that I needed to dig the ditch deeper. After adding to its depth, as bidden, I tried to take a break but, yet again, he kept ordering me to dig and not to cease from my toil. Finally, after commanding me a third and fourth time to do the same, he said the depth was sufficient and told me to build the rest without toil since the toil was done and the construction would proceed without toil."[6] To this prediction the events bear witness, for what ended up happening went beyond Nature.

Moving on from there he next took up lodging with some ascetics who lived nearby. After spending two years with them, he became enamored of the more perfect virtue and took up residence in the village of Teleda, where the great and godly men Ammianus and Eusebius had established their

νυν παρ' ἐκείνοις διατρίψας χρόνον εἰς Τελάνισ-
σον ἀφίκετο κώμην, τῇ κορυφῇ ἐφ' ἧς νῦν ἔστηκεν
ὑποκειμένη. Ἐν ταύτῃ μικρὸν οἰκίστον εὑρὼν τρία
καθειργμένος διεστέλεσεν ἔτη· αὔξειν δὲ ἀεὶ τῆς
ἀρετῆς τὸν πλοῦτον φιλονεικῶν ἐπεθύμησε Μωυσῇ
καὶ Ἠλιᾷ τοῖς θείοις ἀνθρώποις παραπλησίως
τεσσαράκοντα ἡμέρας ἄσιτος διαμεῖναι. Καὶ πέθει
τὸν θαυμάσιον Βάσσον, ὃς τηνικαῦτα πολλὰς περι-
ώδευε κώμας τοῖς κατὰ κώμην ἱερεῦσιν ἐπιστατῶν,
μηδὲν μὲν ἔνδον καταλιπεῖν, πηλῷ δὲ καταχρῖσαι
τὴν θύραν. Τοῦ δὲ καὶ τὴν δυσκολίαν τοῦ πράγματος ὑπαγορεύοντος καὶ παραινοῦντος μὴ νομίζειν
ἀρετὴν εἶναι τὸν βίαιον θάνατον—κατηγορία γὰρ
αὕτη καὶ μεγίστη καὶ πρώτη· "Ἀλλὰ σύ γε, ἔφη, ὦ
πάτερ, δέκα μοι ἄρτους καὶ στάμνον ὕδατος ἀπό-
θου, κἂν ἴδω τὸ σῶμα τροφῆς δεόμενον, μεταλή-
ψομαι τούτων." Ἐγένετο ὡς ἐκέλευσε· καὶ τὰ μὲν
ἀπετίθετο, ἡ δὲ θύρα τὸν πηλὸν ὑπεδέχετο. Μετὰ
δὲ τὸ τέλος τῶν ἡμερῶν ἧκε μὲν ὁ θαυμάσιος ἐκεῖνος καὶ τοῦ θεοῦ ἄνθρωπος Βάσσος, τὸν δὲ πηλὸν
ἀφελὼν καὶ τῆς θύρας εἴσω γενόμενος ηὗρε μὲν
τῶν ἄρτων τὸν ἀριθμόν, ηὗρε δὲ πλῆρες τὸ στα-
μνίον τοῦ ὕδατος, αὐτὸν δὲ ἄπνουν ἐρριμμένον καὶ
οὔτε φθέγγεσθαι οὔτε κινεῖσθαι δυνάμενον. Σπογ-
γιὰν τοίνυν αἰτήσας καὶ ταύτῃ τὸ στόμα διαβρέξας
καὶ ἀποκλύσας προσήνεγκεν αὐτῷ τῶν θείων μυ-

wrestling-school for ascetics.[7] . . . He stayed with them a short time and then went to the village of Telanissus, at the foot of the hilltop where he now stands. Here he found a small cottage and lived in confinement for three years. Always striving ever to increase his rich store of virtue, he desired to subsist without food for forty days like God's men Moses and Elijah. So, he persuaded the amazing Bassus, who used to make the rounds to many villages as overseer of village priests, to leave nothing inside the cottage and seal the door with mud. When Bassus suggested the difficulty of the deed and exhorted him not to think suicide a virtue—for that is the foremost and greatest crime—Symeon replied, "So then, father, set out for me ten loaves of bread and a jug of water. If I see my body needs food, I'll partake of them." It was done as he directed: The food was laid out and the door sealed with mud. At the end of the forty days the amazing Bassus, a person of God, came back, removed the mud, and once inside the door found the same number of loaves and the jug of water full. Symeon, though, lay stretched out and wasn't breathing and was unable to speak or move. Bassus then called for a sponge to soak and rinse Symeon's mouth, then administered to him the tokens of the divine mysteries.

στηρίων τὰ σύμβολα. Καὶ οὕτω διὰ τούτων ἀναρ-
ρωσθεὶς ἀνέστησέ τε ἑαυτὸν καὶ τροφῆς τινος με-
τρίας μετέλαβε, θριδακίνας καὶ σέρεις καὶ τὰ
τούτοις παραπλήσια κατὰ βραχὺ διαμασώμενος
καὶ τῇ γαστρὶ παραπέμπων. ...

Ἐξ ἐκείνου τοίνυν μέχρις καὶ τήμερον—ὀκτὼ δὲ
καὶ εἴκοσι διελήλυθεν ἔτη—τὰς τετταράκοντα
ἄσιτος διαμένει ἡμέρας. Ὁ δὲ χρόνος καὶ ἡ μελέτη
τοῦ πόνου τὸ πλέον ἐσύλησεν. Εἰώθει μὲν γὰρ τὰς
πρώτας ἡμέρας ἑστάναι καὶ τὸν θεὸν ἀνυμνεῖν, εἶτα
τοῦ σώματος διὰ τὴν ἀπαστίαν φέρειν οὐκ ἔτι τὴν
στάσιν ἰσχύοντος καθῆσθαι λοιπὸν καὶ τὴν θείαν
λειτουργίαν ἐπιτελεῖν. τὰς δὲ τελευταίας ἡμέρας καὶ
προσκλίνεσθαι· δαπανωμένης γὰρ κατὰ βραχὺ τῆς
ἰσχύος καὶ ἀποσβεννυμένης κεῖσθαι ἡμιθανὴς ἠναγ-
κάζετο, ἐμηχανήσατο δὲ τὴν στάσιν ἑτέρως. Δοκὸν
γάρ τινα προσδήσας τῷ κίονι καὶ σχοινίοις πάλιν
ἑαυτὸν τῇ δοκῷ προσαρμόσας τὰς τετταράκοντα
οὕτω διετέλεσεν ἡμέρας. Μετὰ δὲ ταῦτα πλείονος
λοιπὸν τῆς ἄνωθεν χάριτος ἀπολαύσας οὐδὲ ταύτης
ἐδεήθη τῆς βοηθείας, ἀλλ' ἕστηκε τὰς τετταράκοντα ἡμέρας σιτίων μὲν οὐκ ἀπολαύων, προθυμίᾳ
δὲ καὶ θείᾳ ῥωννύμενος χάριτι.

And so, his strength revived by these, he sat himself up and took a bit of food—some lettuce, chicory, and similar vegetables—which he chewed into small pieces and swallowed into his stomach. . . .

Twenty-eight years have passed from that time till today and he still perseveres forty days without food. Time and practice have removed most of the hardship: For the first period of days he'd sing hymns to God standing; later, when his body no longer had the strength to endure a standing posture, he'd perform the divine liturgy seated for a spell; for the final stretch of days he'd lie prostrate, for as his strength was gradually being spent and extinguished, he was forced to lie down half-dead. However, when he took his stand upon the column, he would not permit himself to come down, so he contrived to maintain a standing posture by different means: He fastened a kind of beam to the column, tied himself to the beam with ropes, and thus completed the forty days. Since that time going forward, enjoying more grace from above, he has not needed even this assistance, but stands the forty days, not by availing himself of food but strengthened by zeal and divine grace.

Τρία τοίνυνμ ὡς ἔφην, ἐν ἐκείνῳ τῷ οἰκίσκῳ δι-
ατελέσας ἔτη τὴν πολυθρύλητον ταύτην κατέλαβε
κορυὴν θριγκίον ἐν κύκλῳ γενέσθαι παρεγγυήσας,
ἄλυσιν δὲ ἐκ σιδήρου πήχεων εἴκοσι κατασκευάσας
καὶ ταύτης θατέραν μὲν ἀρχὴν πέτρᾳ τινὶ μεγίστῃ
προσηλώσας, θατέραν δὲ τῷ δεξιῷ ποδὶ προσαρμόσας, ὡς ἂν μηδὲ βουλόμενος ἔξω τῶν ὅρων
ἐκείνων ἀπίοι, ἔνδον διῆγεν διηνεκῶς τὸν οὐρανὸν
φανταζόμενος καὶ τὰ ἄνω τῶν οὐρανῶν θεωρεῖν
βιαζόμενος· οὐ γὰρ ἐκώλυε τῆς διανοίας τὴν πτῆ-
σιν ὁ τοῦ σιδήρου δεσμός. Ἐπειδὴ δὲ Μελέτιος ὁ
θαυμάσιος ἐπισκοπεῖν τηνικαῦτα τῆς Ἀντιόχου
πόλεως τεταγμένος τὴν χώραν, ἀνὴρ φρενήρης
καὶ συνέσει λάμπων καὶ ἀγχινοίᾳ κεκοσμημένος,
περιττὸν ἔφη τὸν σίσηρον ἀρκούσης τῆς γνώμης
λογικὰ τῷ σώματι περιθεῖναι δεσμά, εἶξε μὲν καὶ
τὴν παραίνεσιν εὐπειθῶς εἰσεδέξατο, χαλκέα δὲ
κληθῆναι κελεύσας λῦσαι προσέταξε τὸν δεσμόν.
Ἐπειδὴ δὲ καὶ δέρμα τῷ σκέλει προσήρμοστο, ὡς
ἂν μὴ λωβηθείη ὑπὸ τοῦ σιδήρου τὸ σῶμα, καὶ ἔδει
καὶ τούτου—συνερραμμένον γὰρ ἦν—διαρραγῆναι,
πλείους ἢ εἴκοσι μεγίστους κόρεις ἔφασαν ἐν ἐκείνῳ

As I said, he spent three years at that cottage before taking up residence on that celebrated hilltop where he ordered a circular enclosure to be made. He then got himself an iron chain of twenty cubits, nailed one end of it to a huge rock and fastened the other end to his right foot so that even if he wanted to, he couldn't go beyond the perimeter. He spent his days within this area dreaming of heaven and pressing himself to contemplate what exists above the heavens, for the iron bond did not prevent his thoughts from soaring. When the amazing Meletius, who at that time had been appointed to oversee the region around the city of Antioch and was a sensible, bright, intelligent man, bedecked with shrewdness, told him that the iron was superfluous since the mind suffices to hem in the body by the chain of reason, Symeon relented and readily took the advice: He ordered a smith to be summoned and directed him to release the bond. A piece of leather had been fitted to his leg so that his flesh wouldn't be harmed by the chain. This, too, had to be broken apart, since it had been sewn together and, when it was, people say they saw more than twenty enormous bugs lurking underneath it. Meletius said he saw this, too. I have mentioned the detail to highlight, even from this example, Syme-

κατιδεῖν ἐμφωλεύοντας. Καὶ τοῦτο ἔφη ὁ θαυμάσιος τεθεᾶσθαι Μελέτιος. Ἐγὼ δὲ ἀπεμνημόνευσα
τὴν πολλὴν κἀντεῦθεν τοῦ ἀνδρὸς καρτερίαν ἐπι-
δείκνυς· πιλῆσαι γὰρ τῇ χειρὶ τὸ δέρμα καὶ δια-
φθεῖραι πάντας ῥᾳδίως δυνάμενος τῶν ἀνιαρῶν
δηγμάτων ἠνείχετο καρτερῶν ἐν τοῖς μικροῖς τὴν
τῶν μειζόνων ἀγώνων ἀσπαζόμενος γυμνασίαν.

Τῆς τοίνυν φήμης πάντοσε διαθεούσης συνέθεον
ἅπαντες, οὐχ οἱ γειτονεύοντες μόνοι, ἀλλὰ καὶ οἱ
πολλῶν ἡμερῶν ἀφεστηκότες ὁδόν· οἱ μὲν παρειμέ-
νους τὸ σῶμα προσφέροντες, οἱ δὲ ἀρρώστοις ὑγι-
είαν αἰτοῦντες, οἱ δὲ πατέρες γενέσθαι παρακαλοῦ-
ντες καί, ὃ παρὰ τῆς φύσεως οὐκ ἔλαβον, ἱκέτευον
δι᾽ ἐκείνου λαβεῖν. Λαμβάνοντες δὲ καὶ τῶν αἰτή-
σεων ἀπολαύοντες μετ᾽ εὐφροσύνης μὲν ἐπανῇεσαν
κηρύττοντες δὲ τὰς εὐεργεσίας, ὧν ἔτυχον, πολλα-
πλασίους τῶν αὐτῶν δεησομένους ἐξέπεμπον. Οὕτω
δὲ πάντων πανταχόθεν ἀφικνουμένων καὶ πάσης
ὁδοῦ ποταμὸν μιμουμένης πέλαγος ἀνθρώπων ἔστιν
ἰδεῖν ἐν ἐκείνῳ συνιστάμενον τῷ χωρίῳ τοὺς πανταχόθεν δεχόμενον ποτάμους. Οὐ γὰρ μόνον οἱ τὴν
καθ᾽ ἡμᾶς οἰκουμένην οἰκοῦντες συρρέουσιν, ἀλλὰ
καὶ Ἰσμαηλῖται καὶ Ὁμηρῖται καὶ οἱ ἐκείνων ἐνδότε-

on's considerable self-mastery: He could easily have pressed the leather anklet with his hand and killed all the bugs. Instead, he exercised self-control and endured their painful bites, welcoming in small matters the training for greater contests.

By now his fame was spreading all over and everyone ran to see him, not only neighboring peoples, but also people located many days' journey away. Some brought in the paralyzed, others sought health for the sick, and still others asked to become fathers. They sought by supplication to receive from Symeon what they hadn't received from Nature. When people got what they requested, they were satisfied and returned home with joy. They would spread the word about the benefactions they had secured and sent out many more others to ask for the same things. With all those people now arriving from all directions, every road resembled a river. It was like looking at a sea of humanity stationed in that place, with rivers flowing into the sea on all sides. It wasn't just inhabitants who live in our region that were streaming in. Ishmaelites[8] and Persians and Armenians subject to them, Iberians, Homerites,[9] and people living deeper in the interior washed in too. Many people from the Western fringes came as well—Spaniards, Britons,

ροι. Ἀφίκοντο δὲ πολλοὶ τὰς τῆς ἑσπέρας οἰκοῦντες ἐσχατιάς, Σπάνοι τε καὶ Βρεττανοὶ καὶ Γαλάται οἱ τὸ μέσον τούτων κατέχοντες. Περὶ γὰρ Ἰταλίας περιττὸν καὶ λέγειν. Φασὶ γὰρ οὕτως ἐν Ῥώμῃ τῇ μεγίστῃ πολυθρύλητον γενέσθαι τὸν ἄνδρα, ὡς ἐν ἅπασι τοῖς τῶν ἐργαστηρίων προπυλαίοις εἰκόνας αὐτῷ βραχείας ἀναστηλῶσαι, φυλακήν τινα σφίσιν αὐτοῖς καὶ ἀσφάλειαν ἐντεῦθεν πορίζοντας.

Ἐπειδὴ τοίνυν ἀριθμοῦ κρείττους οἱ ἀφικνούμενοι προσψαύειν δὲ ἅπαντες ἐπεχείρουν καί τινα εὐλογίαν ἀπὸ τῶν δερματίνων ἐκείνων ἱματίων τρυγᾶν, πρῶτον μὲν τῆς τιμῆς τὸ ὑπερβάλλον ἄτοπον εἶναι νομίζων, ἔπειτα καὶ τοῦ πράγματος τὸ ἐπίπονον δυσχεραίνων τὴν ἐπὶ τοῦ κίονος ἐμηχανήσατο στάσιν, πρῶτον μὲν ἐξ πήχεων τμηθῆναι κελεύσας, εἶτα δύο καὶ δέκα, μετὰ δὲ ταῦτα δύο καὶ εἴκοσι, νῦν δὲ ἓξ καὶ τριάκοντα· ἀναπνῆναι γὰρ εἰς οὐρανὸν ἐφίεται καὶ τῆς ἐπιγείου ταύτης ἀπαλλαγῆναι διατριβῆς.

Ἐγὼ δὲ οὐδὲ τῆς θείας ἄνευ οἰκονομίας ταύτην ὑπολαμβάνων γεγενῆσθαι τὴν στάσιν, οὗπερ εἵνεκα τοὺς μεμψιμοίρους παρακαλῶ χαλινῶσαι τὴν γλῶτταν καὶ μὴ ἐπιτρέπειν ὡς ἔτυχε φέρεσθαι σκοπεῖν δὲ

and the Gauls who inhabit the land between them. It's superfluous to speak of Italy. They say that Symeon has become so popular in Rome, that mightiest of cities, that craftsmen have erected small likenesses of him at all the entrances to their workshops to provide safety and security for themselves.

By now the visitors were beyond counting. Everyone kept trying to touch him and reap some blessing from his clothes, which were made of hides. At first, he deemed the excess of honor strange. Later, annoyed at how burdensome the situation had become, he devised his method of standing on a column. At first, he directed a column to be cut off at six cubits, then at twelve, later at twenty-two, and now at thirty-six, for he longs to fly to heaven and be delivered from this earthly life. For my part, I do not think his column-standing came about without a divine plan. I therefore call on the critics to rein in their tongues and not let them run amok to be carried where they will. Consider, rather, how very often the Lord has contrived such stunts for the benefit of those who live at greater ease. He instructed Isaiah to walk about naked and barefoot.[10] He directed Jeremiah to put a loincloth around his waist and in this guise

ὡς πολλάκις τοιαῦτα ὁ δεσπότης τῶν ῥαθυμοτέρων εἵνεκεν ὠφελείας ἐμηχανήσατο. Καὶ γὰρ τὸν Ἡσαΐαν γυμνὸν καὶ ἀνυπόδητον βαδίσαι προσέταξε, καὶ τὸν Ἰερεμίαν περίζωμα τῇ ὀσφύι περιθεῖναι καὶ οὕτω τοῖς ἀπειθέσι προσφέρειν τὴν προφητείαν, καὶ ἄλλοτε δὲ κλοιοὺς ξυλίνους καὶ σιδηροῦς μετὰ ταῦτα τῷ τραχήλῳ περιβαλεῖν· καὶ τῷ Ὡσῆὲ γυναῖκα πόρνην λαβεῖν, καὶ αὖθις ἀγαπῆσαι γυναῖκα πονηρὰν καὶ μοιχαλίδα· καὶ τῷ Ἰεζεκιὴλ ἐπὶ τοῦ δεξιοῦ πλευροῦ τεσσαράκοντα κατακλιθῆναι ἡμέρας καὶ ἐπὶ τοῦ εὐωνύμου πεντήκοντα καὶ ἑκατόν· καὶ πάλιν διορύξαι τοῖχον καὶ φεύγοντα ἐξελθεῖν, καὶ αἰχμαλωσίαν ἐν ἑαυτῷ διαγράψαι· καὶ ἄλλοτε δὲ ξίφος εἰς ἀκμὴν παραθῆξαι καὶ ξυρᾶσθαι τούτῳ τὴν κεφαλὴν καὶ τετραχῇ τὰς τρίχας διελεῖν καὶ ἀπονεῖμαι τὰς μὲν εἰς τόδε, τὰς δὲ εἰς τόδε ἵνα μὴ ἅπαντα κατελέγω. Γίνεσθαι δὲ τούτων ἕκαστον προσέταττε τῶν ὅλων ὁ πρύτανις, τοὺς λόγῳ μὴ πειθομένους μηδὲ τῆς προφετείας ἐπαΐειν ἀνεχομένους τῷ τῆς θεωρίας παραδόξῳ συλλέγων καὶ τῶν θεσπισμάτων ἀκούειν παρασκευάζων. Τίς γὰρ οὐκ ἂν ἐξεπλάγη θεῖον ἄνθρωπον γυμνὸν βαδίζοντα θεωρῶν; Τίς δαὶ οὐκ ἂν τοῦ γιγνομένου μαθεῖν τὴν αἰτίαν ἐπόθησε; Τίς

to deliver his prophecy to the unbelieving.[11] On another occasion God told Jeremiah to put a wooden collar on his neck and, afterwards, one made of iron.[12] He directed Hosea to take a prostitute as wife and, moreover, to love her—a prostitute and adulteress.[13] Ezekiel he told to lie on his right side for forty days and on his left for one hundred and fifty;[14] to tunnel through a wall and exit as a fugitive, inscribing in his person the Captivity;[15] to sharpen the blade of his sword, shave his head with it, and to separate the hair into four portions to distribute for various purposes (so that I need not describe each one).[16] The Governor of the universe directed that each of these actions be done to attract, by the unexpectedness of a spectacle, those who would not obey a word or who resisted heeding a prophecy and to get them to pay attention to divine pronouncements. For who would not have been shocked at seeing a man of God parading around naked? Who would not have yearned to know the cause of it happening? Who would not have asked why indeed a prophet let himself cohabitate with a prostitute? Just as the God of the universe arranged for each of those actions to be performed because He was eager to help people accustomed to a life of ease, so too has He decreed

δαὶ οὐκ ἂν ἤρετο τί δήποτε πόρνῃ συνοικεῖν ὁ προ-
φήτης ἀνέχεται; Καθάπερ τοίνυν ἐκείνων ἕκαστον
ὁ τῶν ὅλων θεὸς γενέσθαι προσέταξε τῆς τῶν ῥα-
στώνῃ συζώντων προμηθούμενος ὠφελείας, οὕτω
καὶ τὸ καινὸν τοῦτο καὶ παράδοξον ἐπρυτάνευσε
θέαμα τῷ ξένῳ πάντας ἕλκων εἰς θεωρίαν καὶ πιν-
θανὴν τοῖς ἀφικνουμένοις παρασκευάζων τὴν προ-
σφερομένην παραίνεσιν· τὸ γὰρ καινὸν τοῦ θεάμα-
τος ἐνέχυρον ἀξιόχρεων γίνεται τοῦ διδάγματος,
καὶ ὁ εἰς θεωρίαν ἀφικνούμενος τὰ θεῖα παιδευθεὶς
ἐπανέρχεται. Καὶ ὥσπερ οἱ βασιλεύειν τῶν ἀνθρώπων λαχόντες ἀμείβουσι κατά τινα χρόνου περίο-
δον τὰς τῶν νομισμάτων εἰκόνας, ποτὲ μὲν λεόντων
ἐκτυποῦντες ἰνδάλματα, ποτὲ δὲ ἀστέρων καὶ ἀγ-
γέλων, ἄλλοτε τῷ ξένῳ χαρακτῆρι τιμιώτερον ἀπο-
φαίνειν πειρώμενος τὸν χρυσόν, οὕτως ὁ τῶν ὅλων
παμβασιλεὺς οἷόν τινας χαρακτῆρας τὰς καινὰς
ταύτας καὶ παντοδαπὰς πολιτείας τῇ εὐσεβείᾳ περι-
τιθεὶς οὐ μόνον τῶν τροφίμων τῆς πίστεως, ἀλλὰ
καὶ τῶν τὴν ἀπιστίαν νοσούντων εἰς εὐφημίαν τὰς
γλώττας κινεῖ.

· · · · · ·

Ἐγὼ δὲ αὐτοῦ πρὸ τούτων ἁπάντων τὴν καρτερίαν θαυμάζων. Νύκτωρ γὰρ καὶ μεθ᾽ ἡμέραν ἕστηκεν ὑπὸ πάντων ὁρώμενος· τὰς θύρας γὰρ ἀφελὼν
καὶ τοῦ περιβόλου μέρος οὐκ ἐλάχιστον καταλύ-

this new and unexpected spectacle to draw everyone to look at it while contriving to make the advice offered to visitors persuasive. For the novelty of the spectacle becomes a reliable guarantee of the teaching, and the person who came only to look still departs instructed in theology. Those who have been allotted kingship over people change the images on coins from time to time. Sometimes they strike depictions of lions, sometimes stars and angels. At other times they try to make a gold piece look more valuable by placing an unusual stamp on it. Just so the All-King of the universe has conferred on piety, as if He were striking coins, a new and various social currency[17] and moves tongues to a profession of faith, not only the tongues of those reared in belief, but also of those sick with disbelief.

[Theodoret continues (sections 13–21) with an account of the conversion of various of Symeon's visitors as well as his miracles and prophecies.]

More than all that, however, I personally admire his strength of will. He stands night and day in view of all. He removed the doors and demolished a none too small part of the enclosure, so he is on display to everyone, a strange and extraordinary sight, now standing for quite some time, now of-

σας, πρόκειται πᾶσι θέαμα καινὸν καὶ παράδοξον, νῦν μὲν ἑστὼς μέχρι πολλοῦ, νῦν δὲ θαμὰ κατακαμπτόμενος καὶ τῷ θεῷ προσφέρων προσκύνησιν. Πολλοὶ δὲ καὶ ἀριθμοῦσι τῶν ἑστώτων ταυτασὶ τὰς προσκυνήσεις. Ἅπαξ δέ τις τῶν σὺν ἐμοὶ χιλίας καὶ διακοσίας πρὸς τέτταρσι καὶ τεσσαράκοντα ἀριθμήσας, εἶτα ὀκλάσας ἀφῆκε τὴν ψῆφον. Κατακύπτων δὲ ἀεὶ τοῖς τῶν ποδῶν δακτύλοις προσεπελάζει τὸ μέτωπον· ἅπαξ γὰρ τῆς ἑβδομάδος τροφὴν ἡ γαστὴρ ὑποδεχομένη καὶ ταύτην βραχεῖαν εὐπετῶς ἐπικάμπτεσθαι τῷ νώτῳ παραχωρεῖ.

Φασὶ δὲ ἀπὸ τῆς στάσεως καὶ χειρώνειον ἕλκος ἐν θατέρῳ γενέσθαι ποδὶ καὶ διηνεκῶς πλεῖστον ἐκεῖθεν ἰχῶρα ἐκκρίνεσθαι. Ἀλλ᾽ ὅμως οὐδὲν τουτωνὶ τῶν παθῶν τὴν φιλοσοφίαν ἐξήλεγξεν, ἀλλὰ φέρει γενναίως καὶ τὰ ἑκουσία καὶ τὰ ἀκουσία, καὶ τούτων κἀκείνων τῇ προθυμίᾳ περιγινόμενος. Τοῦτο δὲ τὸ ἕλκος καὶ ὑποδεῖξαί τινι ἠναγκάσθη ποτέ. Διηγήσομαι δὲ καὶ τὴν αἰτίαν.

Ἀφίκετό τις ἀπὸ Ῥαβαίνης, ἀνὴρ σπουδαῖος καὶ τῇ τοῦ Χριστοῦ διακονίᾳ τετιμημένος. Οὗτος τὴν κορυφὴν ἐκείνην καταλαβών· "Εἰπέ μοι, ἔφη, πρὸς τῆς ἀληθείας αὐτῆς τῆς τὸ τῶν ἀνθρώπων πρὸς

fering worship to God by bending down repeatedly. Many of the people standing by count the number of these bows. One time a person with me counted one thousand two hundred and forty-four of them, at which point he slackened and gave up counting. When Symeon bends down, his forehead always touches his toes. The fact that his stomach takes in food only once a week and only a little at that allows him to bend at the back easily.

They say that because of his standing a sore in need of attention has developed on his left foot and a great deal of puss oozes out of it continually. And yet none of these sufferings has confounded his philosophy. He endures them with nobility, both the ones he has chosen voluntarily and those that are involuntary, conquering both kinds by his zeal. One time he was compelled to show this sore to someone. I shall explain the reason.

A certain man arrived from Rabaena. He was an earnest person, having been honored as one of Christ's deacons. When he reached the top of the hill, he said, "Tell me, swearing by the very Truth that has turned humankind toward Itself, are you a human or a nature without a body?" Those present were annoyed at the question, but Symeon told them to keep quiet and said to the man, "Why ever

ἑαυτὴν ἐπιστρεψάσης γένος, ἄνθρωπος εἶ ἢ ἀσώ-
ματος φύσις;” Δυσκερανάντων δὲ πρὸς τὴν ἐρώ-
τησιν τῶν παρόντων σιγὴν ἄγειν ἐκέλευσεν ἅπαντας, πρὸς ἐκεῖνον δὲ ἔφη “Τί δήποτε ταύτην τὴν
πεῦσιν προσήνεγκας;” Τοῦ δὲ εἰρηκότος ὡς “πάντων θηλούντων ἀκούω ὡς οὔτε ἐσθίεις οὔτε
καθεύδεις, ἀνθρώπων δὲ ἑκάτερον ἴδιον· οὐ γὰρ
ἄν τις ταύτην ἔχων τὴν φύσιν τροφῆς δίχα καὶ ὕπνου
διαβιώσειεν”, ἐπιτεθῆναι μὲν τῷ κίονι κλίμακα
προσέταξεν, ἀναβῆναι δὲ ἐκεῖνον ἐκέλευσε καὶ
πρῶτον μὲν τὰς χεῖρας καταμαθεῖν εἶτα εἴσω τοῦ
δερματίνου περιβολαίου τὴν χεῖρα βαλεῖν καὶ ἰδεῖν
μὴ τοὺς πόδας μόνον, ἀλλὰ καὶ τὸ χαλεπώτατον
ἕλκος. Ἰδὼν δὲ καὶ θαυμάσας ὁ ἄνθρωπος τὴν τοῦ
ἕλκους ὑπερβολὴν καὶ παρ' αὐτοῦ μαθὼν ὡς ἀπο-
λαύει τροφῆς, κατελήλυθεν μὲν ἐκεῖθεν, πρὸς ἐμὲ
δὲ ἀφικόμενος διηγήσατο ἅπαντα.

Ἐν δὲ ταῖς δημοτελέσι πανηγύρεσι καὶ ἄλλην
ἐπιδείκνυται καρτερίαν. Μετὰ γὰρ ἡλίου δυσμὰς
ἕως ἂν οὗτος πάλιν εἰς τὸν ἑῷον ὁρίζοντα γένηται,
τὰς χεῖρας ἀνατείνων εἰς οὐρανὸν παννύχιον
ἕστηκεν οὔτε ὑπὸ ὕπνου θελγόμενος οὔτε ὑπὸ πόνου
νικώμενος.

Ἐν τοσούτοις δὲ πόνοις καὶ κατορθωμάτων ὄγκῳ
καὶ πλήθει θαυμάτων οὕτως ἐστὶ τὸ φρόνημα μέ-
τριος ὡς πάντων ἀνθρώπων κατὰ τὴν ἀξίαν ὕστα-

have you posed this question?" He replied, "I hear everyone chattering about how you don't eat or lie down to sleep, both of which are normal for humans. A person with human nature could not live without food and sleep." At that Symeon gave instructions for a ladder to be placed against the column and told the man to climb up—first, to examine his hands, and then to place his own hand inside his cloak of hides, and to inspect not only his feet, but that most grievous sore as well. Once he had seen and marveled at the excessiveness of the sore and having learned that Symeon does in fact eat food, the man climbed down from there, came over to me and recounted everything.

During the public festivals Symeon displays another feat of strength. From the setting of the sun until it rises again in the East he extends his hands to heaven and stands all night, neither lulled to sleep nor bested by exertion.

Amidst so many feats of endurance, a mass of good deeds, and an abundance of miracles, Symeon is as modest in spirit as if he were the last of all people in worth. In addition to his modest spirit he is very approachable, pleasant, and charming. He answers everyone who engages him in conversation, whether it be an artisan, a beggar, or a rustic.

τος. Πρὸς δὲ τῷ μετρίῳ φρονήματι καὶ εὐπρόσοδος
λίαν ἐστὶ καὶ γλυκὺς καὶ ἐπίχαρις καὶ πρὸς ἕκαστον
τῶν διαλεγομένων ἀποκρινόμενος, εἴτε χειροτέ-
χνης εἴτε προσαίτης εἴτε ἄγροικος εἴη. Ἔλαβε δὲ
καὶ τῆς διδασκαλίας παρὰ τοῦ μεγαλοδώρου δεσπότου τὸ δῶρον· καὶ δὶς ἑκάστης ἡμέρας τὰς πα-
ραινέσεις ποιούμενος ἐπικλύζει τῶν ἀκουόντων
τὰς ἀκοὰς ἐπιχαρίτως μάλα διαλεγόμενος, καὶ τὰ
τοῦ θείου πνεύματος προσφέρων παιδεύματα καὶ
ἀνανεύειν εἰς οὐρανὸν καὶ πέτεσθαι παρεγγυῶν καὶ
τῆς γῆς ἀπαλλάττεσθαι καὶ τὴν προσδοκωμένην
φαντάζεσθαι βασιλείαν καὶ τῆς γεέννης δεδιέναι
τὴν ἀπειλὴν καὶ καταφρονεῖν τῶν γηΐνων καὶ προ-
σμένειν τὰ μέλλοντα.

Ἔστι δὲ αὐτὸν ἰδεῖν καὶ δικάζοντα καὶ ὀρθὰς καὶ
δικαίας τὰς ψήφους ἐκφέροντα. Ταῦτα δὲ καὶ τὰ
τοιαῦτα μετὰ τὴν ἐνάτην διαπράττεται ὥραν· τὴν
γὰρ νύκτα ἅπασαν καὶ ἡμέραν μέχρις ἐνάτης δια-
τελεῖ προσευχόμενος. Μετὰ δὲ τὴν ἐνάτην πρῶτον
μὲν τὴν θείαν διδασκαλίαν τοῖς παροῦσι προσφέ-
ρει, εἶτα τὴν ἑκάστου δεξάμενος αἴτησιν καί τινας
ἰάσεις ἐργασάμενος τῶν ἀμφισβητούντων διαλύει
τὰς ἔριδας. Περὶ δὲ ἡλίου δυσμὰς τῆς πρὸς τὸν θεὸν
λοιπὸν διαλέξως ἄρχεται. . . .

Ταῦτα δὲ διεξῆλθον ἀπὸ ψεκάδος δεῖξαι τὸν
ὑετὸν πειραθεὶς καὶ τῷ λιχανῷ δακτύλῳ τοὺς

He has received, too, the gift of teaching from our generous Lord. He floods the ears of his audience with exhortations twice a day, conversing with exceeding grace and offering the teachings of the divine Spirit. He enjoins people to look to heaven, quit the earth, and fly away, to picture to themselves the kingdom they expect to inherit, to dread the threats of Hell, to despise earthly things, and to await what is to come.

One can also watch him rendering judgements and issuing verdicts that are upright and just. He busies himself with these and similar tasks after the ninth hour,[18] for until then he spends the whole night and day in prayer. But after the ninth hour, his first task is to provide divine instruction to the people present; then, he receives the requests of each and performs various cures before resolving the disagreements of those at odds. Around sunset he begins his conversation with God for the remainder of the evening. . . .

I have gone through these details, trying, as it were, for those who might stumble upon my treatise, to point out a rain shower from a rain drop, and with my forefinger to give a taste of the honey's sweetness. The stories on the lips of all are far more numerous than these. But I did not promise

ἐντυγχάνοντας τῷ συγγράμματι τῆς γλυκύτητος ἀπογεύων τοῦ μέλιτος. Τὰ δὲ παρὰ πάντων ἀδόμενα τούτων ἐστὶ πολλαπλάσια, ἀλλ' οὐ πάντα ἔγωγε συγγράφειν ἐπήγγελμαι, ἀλλὰ δι' ὀλίγων τῆς ἑκάστου πολιτείας ἐπιδεῖξαι τὸν χαρακτῆρα. Συγγράψουσι δὲ ὡς εἰκὸς καὶ ἄλλοι τουτωνὶ πολλῷ πλείονα· εἰ δὲ καὶ ἐπιβιῴη, καὶ μείζονα τυχὸν προσθήσουσι θαύματα. Ἐγὼ δὲ καὶ αὐτὸν ταῖς οἰκείαις προσευχαῖς βοηθούμενον τοῖς ἀγαθοῖς τούτοις πόνοις ἐπινμεῖναι καὶ ποθῶ καὶ τῆς εὐσεβείας ἀγλάϊσμα καὶ τὸν ἐμαυτοῦ ῥυθμισθῆναι βίον καὶ τὴν εὐαγγελικὴν πολιτείαν κατευθυνθῆναι.

to record everything, only to show from a few examples the character and constitution of each thing. Others are bound to chronicle more material than this by far, and, if Symeon lives on, they will perhaps add greater miracles. As for me, what I yearn and beg from God is that Symeon, helped by his own prayers, will continue in these good works, for he is an ornament of piety we all share. And may my own life be patterned and set aright according to the Gospel's rules for living.

NOTES

Introduction

1. *Iliad* 1.149–157. The foot soldier Thersites is another model recalcitrant (*Iliad* 2.211–277).

2. Plato, *Apology* 38a.

3. Diogenes Laertius 6.35.

4. See selection no. 1.

5. See selection no. 9.

6. On this topic, see the seminal piece by Thomas McEvilley, "Diogenes of Sinope (ca. 410–ca. 320 B.C.): Selected Performance Pieces," *ArtForum* 21, no. 7 (1983): pp. 58–59.

7. See Diogenes Laertius's comments in selection no. 1.

8. www.mrmoneymustache.com.

9. www.colinbeavan.com.

10. Odell expresses admiration for Diogenes on pages 64–69 of her book.

11. The concept was developed by E. F. Schumacher in the 1950s and 60s while working as chief economist for the British National Coal Board and as a consultant to former British colonies in South Asia (Burma, India). He was heavily influenced by the approach to economic resistance championed by Mohandas Gandhi. Schumacher himself used the term "intermediate technology," by

which he meant a technology superior to inefficient, rudimentary tools and practices, yet one "simpler, cheaper and freer than the supertechnology of the rich." See E. F. Schumacher, *Small Is Beautiful: Economics as if People Mattered* (New York: Harper Perennial, 1989 [1973]), pp. 155–201. See further my *Plato's Pigs and Other Ruminations: Ancient Guides to Living with Nature* (Cambridge: Cambridge University Press, 2020), pp. 134–144.

12. See selection no. 1.

13. Though Seneca argues in selection no. 2 that Cynic antics can turn ordinary people away from philosophy.

14. Even more precisely, my work was supported by the French Institutes for Advanced Study international mobility fellowship scheme under the Marie Skłodowska-Curie grant agreement No. 945408, a European Union's Horizon 2020 research and innovation program.

1. Life Is a Dog (Selections from Diogenes Laertius, *Lives and Opinions of Eminent Philosophers*, Book 6)

1. Diocles of Magnesia (fl. 2nd century BCE) was a precursor to Diogenes Laertius who wrote biographies of philosophers. His work is lost.

2. Euboulides of Miletus (fl. 4th century BCE), a student of Euclid, was a composer of philosophical paradoxes and, as suggested here, a life of Diogenes, now lost.

3. "The Farter." It is unclear if Diogenes wrote such a work—Julian reports the then current view that he did not (see selection no. 9).

4. "Shawm," here and in the passage from Julian (selection no. 9), translates the Greek word *aulos*, a reed in-

strument that sounded like a modern oboe, a muted bag-pipe, or, indeed, a shawm.

5. *Odyssey* 4.392.

6. A fragment from Euripides's lost play the *Antiope*. Euripides fragment 200 in *Fragments: Aegeus-Meleager*, edited and translated by Christopher Collard and Martin Cropp, Loeb Classical Library, Vol. 504 (Cambridge, MA: Harvard University Press, 2008).

7. A "shortcut" because Stoicism involved studying elaborate theories about physics, logic, and human psychology.

8. This sentence, which appears a little later in the same paragraph, seems to have been displaced, so I have transposed it here.

9. A colonnaded temple in the Agora dedicated to Zeus Eleutherios ("The Liberator") built after the Greek victory over the Persians.

10. A public building located in the Kerameikos (the "Potter's Quarter" and site of a public cemetery), where the Panathenaic procession to Eleusis began.

11. A temple in the Agora sacred to the Mother of the Gods, which also served as the depository of Athens' public archives.

12. Combining §§46 and 69.

13. A pun in the Greek on *logos* ("reason") and *brochos* ("noose," or "halter").

14. Literally, "a Citizen of the Universe," but what Diogenes is decrying here is the nativism and provincialism of, for example, "Athenian," "Spartan," or "Boeotian."

15. That Plato is likely the recipient of the question in this anecdote, see Aelian, *Varia Historia* 14.33.

16. A cypress grove on the outskirts of Corinth.
17. Autarky is *autarkeia*, "self-sufficiency," a Cynic virtue.

3. Cynic in Swaddling Clothes
(*Cynic Epistles* 33, Crates, to Hipparchia)

1. Aethra was impregnated with the future Athenian hero and king, Theseus, by Theseus's father Aegeus when Aegeus visited Troezen en route to Athens from Delphi. Before leaving Troezen Aegeus hid his sword and sandals under a large rock with instructions that if Aethra were to deliver a son and were he to reach the age of being able to move the rock and claim his paternal tokens, she should send the boy to join him in Athens to stake his claim as heir to the throne (Plutarch, *Life of Theseus* 3–4). The staff (*baktēria*), cloak (*tribōn*), and knapsack (*pēra*) were characteristic Cynic attributes.

2. The Greeks observed that young storks took care of their aged parents, providing both food and shelter for them. Ancient writers speak of "Stork Laws" (*Nomoi Pelargikoi*; Latin: *Lex Ciconia*) that required citizens to take care of their parents in old age (compare Aristophanes, *Birds* 1353–1355 with D'Arcy Thompson, *A Glossary of Greek Birds* [Oxford: Clarendon Press, 1895], p. 128).

4. My Friend Demetrius
(Seneca, *De Beneficiis* 7.1–2 and 8–11)

1. Selections translated by James S. Romm, *How to Give: An Ancient Guide to Giving and Receiving* (Princeton, NJ: Princeton University Press, 2020).

2. This is a paraphrase of Democritus: "In reality, we know nothing. For the truth lies in an abyss." Democritus D24 in *Early Greek Philosophy, Volume VII: Later Ionian and Athenian Thinkers, Part 2*, edited and translated by André Laks and Glenn W. Most, Loeb Classical Library, Vol. 503 (Cambridge, MA: Harvard University Press, 2016). Compare with Heraclitus's statement that "Nature loves to hide." Heraclitus D35 in *Early Greek Philosophy, Volume III: Early Ionian Thinkers, Part 2*, edited and translated by André Laks and Glenn W. Most, Loeb Classical Library, Vol. 526 (Cambridge, MA: Harvard University Press, 2016).

3. Chrysippus was an important early synthesizer of Stoic doctrines, Zeno the school's founder.

4. A clever wordplay on the verb forms *corrumpi* and *corripi*, the full sense of which is nearly impossible to capture in English. *Corrumpi* can also mean "bribed," which is especially apt given the extended metaphor Seneca is developing in this passage, and *corripi* can mean "robbed." Seneca is implying that 1) Demetrius was impervious to the bad influences of his times (Seneca's own, the reign of Nero), and 2) those times were sufficiently awful not to have followed his good example or advice (*nec nos ab illo corripi*).

5. Murrine glass is the result of a technique that creates colored patterns, like Venetian glasswork from Murano.

6. The idea that a moneylender is selling time (*venale tempus*), an entity that belongs only to God or the universe, appears here possibly for the first time. It became a topos in later vituperations against usury.

5. Student Tribute (Lucian, *Life of Demonax*, abridged)

1.   This work is lost, but Lucian's tantalizing description suggests that in Sostratus there was blended a curious mixture of Robin Hood and Grizzly Adams.

2.   Agathoboulus was a Cynic from Alexandria, Egypt. Demetrius here is not the Cynic of selection no. 4, but a different person, from Sunium. Epictetus is the famous Stoic philosopher. Nothing else is known of Timocrates of Heraclea.

3.   See below on his manner of death.

4.   A fragment from the comic poet Eupolis, referring in the original context to the eloquence of the statesman Pericles. Eupolis fragment 102 in *Fragments of Old Comedy, Volume II: Diopeithes to Pherecrates*, edited and translated by Ian C. Storey, Loeb Classical Library, Vol. 514 (Cambridge, MA: Harvard University Press, 2011).

5.   Anytus and Meletus are the named accusers at Socrates's trial for impiety as recounted in Plato's *Apology*.

6.   These secret rites were celebrated at an Athenian shrine about twelve miles from the city in honor of Demeter and her daughter Persephone/Kore.

7.   Referring to the death sentence the Athenians meted out to Socrates in 399 BCE.

6. A Passage to India (Strabo, *Geography* 15.63–65)

1.   Selections translated in Richard Bett, *How to Keep an Open Mind: An Ancient Guide to Thinking Like a Skeptic* (Princeton, NJ: Princeton University Press, 2021).

2. Calanus became ill en route to Susa and self-immolated there in 323 BCE at the age of 73.

3. Calanus and Mandanis seem to be Sadhus or Shramanas. If so, their chief deity would have been Vishnu, transposed here for a Greek audience as Zeus.

4. Calanus's diatribe here seems to refer to a Kali Yuga, the fourth and last degenerate age of the world cycle in Hindu mythology.

5. The eponymous king of Taxila (real name: Ambhi), the ancient city in the Punjab region (modern Pakistan) where these events are taking place.

7. Best in Show (Dio Chrysostom, Oration 9, "Isthmian Discourse")

1. The Isthmian Games were a Panhellenic athletic contest, like the Olympics, held at the Isthmus of Corinth.

2. Modern Marseille.

3. An ancient Greek city on the north coast of the Black Sea, near modern Odessa in the Ukraine.

4. Not only a fact about ancient honey from the Black Sea (Pontic) region (cf. Pliny, *Natural History* 21.13), but an oblique reference to Diogenes's birthplace in nearby Sinope.

5. The hero Odysseus returned from Troy to Ithaca disguised as a beggar to test who had been loyal to him in his absence. The Suitors—Odysseus's subjects—were feasting in his halls, trying to marry his wife Penelope, and take possession of his kingdom. Their abuse of him is described in the latter half of the *Odyssey*.

6.   The poet of course is Homer, whose regular epithet for Achilles, *podas ōkus* ("swift-footed"), says it all. Achilles was also considered the bravest and best Greek warrior at Troy.

7.   At *Iliad* 22.21, Achilles chases Hector on foot around the walls of Troy three times, in pursuit to avenge the death of his friend Patroclus.

8.   This refers to a disturbing story recounted in its fullest detail by Ovid (*Metamorphoses* 6.424–674). In brief, Tereus, a Thracian king, raped his wife's sister, Philomela, and cut out her tongue. She was turned into a nightingale, he into a hoopoe.

8. Interview with a Cynic (Pseudo-Lucian, *The Cynic*)

1.   The name does not likely refer to an actual person, though an allegory of sorts might be implied in that Lykinos, the attacker, means "wolf-like," whereas Kynikos means "dog-like."

2.   The "you" here is plural. The Cynic's speeches in what follows are not so much an ad hominem attack on Lycinus as a diatribe addressed to all, not unlike Demetrius's harangue in selection no. 5.

3.   In myth, Eriphyle took a bribe of a golden necklace to convince her husband Amphiaraus to join the expedition of the Seven against Thebes, where he was killed.

4.   Referring to the Roman *lectica*, or litter, carried around by slaves through the streets (essentially, a rickshaw without wheels).

5.   A kind of rock snail indigenous to the coastal Levant, mucus from whose glands was used to fabricate purple dye for cloth in antiquity.

6. Early in his mythological career, Theseus performed various benefactory labors, wild and roughly clad like Heracles.

7. Chiron was a mythical half-human, half-horse creature (a so-called centaur), who was the tutor to Achilles.

8. With apologies to LGBTQ readers, a *kinaidos*, or catamite, is a man perceived to be effeminate and a passive sexual partner. The general attitude reflected here is not particular to Cynicism but was a standard slur and trope in antiquity.

9. Know Thyself! (Julian, Oration 6, "To the Uneducated Cynics," abridged)

1. A shrine dedicated to the Mother of the Gods in which public records were kept.

2. These are lost, but appear to have been paratragedies, or paratragic burlesques. The *Pordalus*, mentioned in selection no. 1, is one of the titles that have come down to us. One of Diogenes's favorite quips about himself, as reported by Diogenes Laertius (6.38) and quoted in part by Julian below—"A homeless exile, to his country dead, / A wanderer who begs his daily bread"—is in iambic trimeter, the meter of tragic dialogue, and might well be a quotation.

3. Known as the Laughing Philosopher, Democritus of Abdera was the founder of atomism.

4. Plato, *Symposium* 215b-216a.

5. These appear to have been like Russian *matryoshka* dolls. Sileni were mixanthropic creatures from mythology with human, goat, and horse-like attributes. The idea behind

the comparison is that an ugly or clownish exterior can house an ethical character of precious value.

6. Compare selection no. 6 (A Passage to India).

7. Heraclitus fragment D20 in Laks and Most, *Early Greek Philosophy, Volume III.*

8. Apollo, patron god of the Oracle at Delphi.

9. See selection no. 1.

10. Iamblichus (245–345 CE) was a philosopher of the Neoplatonic school that Julian favored.

11. Plato, *Laws* 730b.

12. Aristotle's school.

13. The founder of Stoicism.

14. *Alcibiades* 1.129a.

15. The Greek says "the same thing" but what Julian means is the *opposite* of what Plato said about the value of the phrase "know thyself," namely that he thinks *nothing* of the opinions of the multitude. Alternatively, Julian could mean that Plato will say "the same thing" as Diogenes might be imagined as saying: that the opinions of the multitude are worth nothing.

16. *Crito* 44c. Socrates says this in reply to Crito's concern about what people will think of him if he doesn't help Socrates get out of prison by using his financial means.

17. Plato, *Epistles* 2.314c. The statement is cryptic, and Julian does not quote it precisely, but Plato seems to mean he views his authorial role as "channeling" Socrates, who wrote nothing, but whom he has immortalized in his dialogues, that is, made "beautiful and young" (the historical Socrates was neither). Plato expatiates on why he thinks writing is inferior to oral discourse in *Epistle 7*.

18. An ironic allusion to Plato, *Protagoras* 314a where Socrates compares traveling sophists like Protagoras unfavorably to peddlers of quack medicines. In Plato's analogy "that most precious possession" is the soul.

19. Plato, *Phaedo* 81a.

20. *Iliad* 5.304.

21. This is probably a reference to Diogenes eating raw octopus (see selection no. 1), which Julian's addressee in this treatise found particularly objectionable and a practice that Julian spends several paragraphs justifying (all omitted in this abridgement). But the statement could just as easily apply to any of Diogenes's more outlandish public behavior.

22. Socrates's friend Chaerephon consulted the Oracle to ask who the wisest person in Greece was. Apollo replied that it was Socrates, who concluded from this that because the god cannot be wrong, he must be wisest only because he knows that he knows nothing. He asks questions, seeks definitions, offers correction, but does not promulgate specific answers. See Plato, *Apology* 21a-e.

23. Plato, *Protagoras* 321a-b.

24. A clinical, euphemistic description of Diogenes's habit of defecating and masturbating in public. See selection no. 1.

25. The Cynic Crates of Thebes.

26. Julian is being sarcastic here. Themistocles was commander of the Athenian fleet that defeated Xerxes at the Battle of Salamis in 480 BCE. Alexander defeated Darius at the Battle of Gaugamela in 331 BCE.

10. The Columnist (Theodoret, *Life of Symeon Stylites*, abridged)

1. The idea of playing a fool for Christ stems from biblical passages like 1 Corinthians 4:10, where the apostle Paul writes, "We are fools for Christ's sake, but ye are wise in Christ; we are weak, but ye are strong; ye are honourable, but we are despised."

2. As ably demonstrated by Derek Krueger, *Symeon the Holy Fool: Leontius's* Life *and the Late Antique City* (Berkeley: University of California Press, 1996).

3. Jean Le Rond D'Alembert (1717–1783): "Every age, and especially our own, stands in need of a Diogenes; but the difficulty is in finding men who have the courage to be one, and men who have patience to endure one." From *Miscellaneous Pieces in Literature, History, and Philosophy by Mr. D'Alembert, Translated from the French* (London, 1764), p. 154.

4. Theodoret was bishop of Cyrrhus, an ancient city close to Antioch.

5. The passage read at church appears to have been the Beatitudes (Matthew 5:3–12), from the Sermon on the Mount.

6. Compare Diogenes's remarks in selection no. 1 and Crates's in selection no. 3 about how subjecting oneself to voluntary toil (*ponos*) makes other things easier. St. Francis of Assisi (1182–1226), another avatar of Diogenes, is reported to have received his calling via a similar figurative charge to (re)build a church.

NOTES

7. "Wrestling-school" (Greek *palaistra*) is a bold choice of term for a monastery, as the Cynics were also fond of athletic metaphors for soul-training. Ammianus and Eusebius here are local Christian monks, not their more famous Late Antique namesakes.

8. Perhaps Nabateans.

9. Inhabitants of the southern tip of Saudi Arabia, modern Yemen.

10. Isaiah 2:2.

11. Jeremiah 1:17.

12. Jeremiah 34:1 and 35:10–14.

13. Hosea 1:2 and 3:1.

14. Ezekiel 4.4–6.

15. Ezekiel 12:4–5.

16. Ezekiel 5:1–4.

17. For the metaphor, compare Diogenes's divine call to "deface the currency" in selection no. 1.

18. Around 3 o'clock in the afternoon.

PASSAGES TRANSLATED

Selection 1 from *Diogenes Laertius, Lives of Eminent Philosophers, Volume II: Books 6–10*, edited by R. D. Hicks, Loeb Classical Library, Vol. 185 (1931)

Selection 2 from *Seneca, Epistles 1–65*, edited by Richard Gummere, Loeb Classical Library Vol. 75 (1917)

Selection 3 from Abraham J. Malherbe, *The Cynic Epistles*, Scholars Press, 1977

Selection 4 from *Seneca, Moral Essays, Volume III*, edited by John W. Basore, Loeb Classical Library, Vol. 310 (1935)

Selection 5 from *Lucian, Volume I*, edited by A. M. Harmon, Loeb Classical Library, Vol. 14 (1913)

Selection 6 from *Strabo, Geography, Volume VII: Books 15–16*, edited by Horace Leonard Jones, Loeb Classical Library, Vol. 241 (1930)

Selection 7 from *Dio Chrysostom, Discourses 1–11*, edited by J. W. Cohoon, Loeb Classical Library Vol. 257 (1932)

Selection 8 from *Lucian, Volume VIII*, edited by M. D. Macleod, Loeb Classical Library, Vol. 432 (1967)

Selection 9 from *Julian, Orations 6–8*, edited by Wilmer Cave Wright, Loeb Classical Library, Vol. 29 (1913)

Selection 10 from *L'histoire religieuse de Théodoret de Cyr*, edited by P. Canivet and A. Leroy-Molinghen, Sources chrétiennes, Éditions du Cerf (1977–79)

SUGGESTIONS FOR
FURTHER READING

Ian Cutler, *Cynicism from Diogenes to Dilbert* (Mc-Farland & Company, 2005)

William Desmond, *The Cynics* (University of California Press, 2008)

Marie-Odile Goudet-Cazé, *Cynicism and Christianity in Antiquity* (Eerdmans, 2019)

Luis E. Navia, *Diogenes the Cynic: The War Against the World* (Humanity Books, 2005)

Jenny Odell, *How to Do Nothing: Resisting the Attention Economy* (Melville House, 2020)

M. D. Usher, *Plato's Pigs and Other Ruminations: Ancient Guides to Living with Nature* (Cambridge University Press, 2020)